Will I Make a Difference?

ROTARY CLUB OF PRINCE RUPERT:

VOLUNTEER SERVICE TO THE COMMUNITY

By

NANCY TAEKO EIDSVIK

A proposal submitted in partial fulfillment of

the requirements for the degree of

MASTER OF ARTS

In

LEADERSHIP AND TRAINING

We accept this proposal as conforming

to the required standard

....
Project Sponsor, Larry Sherman

....
Major Project Supervisor, Marie Graf, MA

....
Committee Chair, P. Gerry Nixon, PhD

ROYAL ROADS UNIVERSITY

March 2008

Will I Make a Difference?

Community Service through Rotary

Nancy Eidsvik, MA

iUniverse, Inc.
Bloomington

Will I Make a Difference?
Community Service through Rotary

iUniverse books may be ordered through booksellers or by contacting:

iUniverse
1663 Liberty Drive
Bloomington, IN 47403
www.iuniverse.com
1-800-Authors (1-800-288-4677)

ISBN: 978-1-4620-4417-7 (sc)
ISBN: 978-1-4620-4419-1 (hc)
ISBN: 978-1-4620-4418-4 (ebk)

Printed in the United States of America

iUniverse rev. date: 12/2/2011

TABLE OF CONTENTS

LIST OF TABLES

LIST OF FIGURES

ABSTRACT

This community-based action research study examined how the Rotary Club of Prince Rupert can best expand its volunteer service to the community. This research opportunity provided members of the Rotary Club and the community to share their impressions and experiences of the Rotary Club. The study offered an avenue for participation in establishing recommendations to strengthen the Rotary Club's presence in the community. Research methods of focus groups, World Café, interviews, and surveys were used. Ethical considerations included confidentiality, free and informed consent, minimizing harm, and maximizing benefits. Recommendations are offered to expand public awareness of the Rotary Club, establish a strategic plan to address organizational effectiveness, and encourage key planning to identify opportunities for volunteer services. The recommendations in this research study can be used by other Rotary Clubs and service organizations to assist them by evaluating and strategizing how to best expand their volunteer services to their communities.

ACKNOWLEDGEMENTS

My sincerest thanks to:

The members of the Rotary Club of Prince Rupert for your continuous support and appreciation.

All the participants who made this research possible—members of the Rotary Club of Prince Rupert, members of the Hecate Strait Rotary Club, Mayor and City Councillors, and all service provider organizations who responded to my request for input.

Larry Sherman, project sponsor, for his enthusiasm and commitment to my project.

Marie Graf, project supervisor, for her intuition in understanding my needs, never imposing on me, but always saying the right things at the right moment.

Karen Graham, editor, for her timely responses to my call for help and her ever respectful manner when giving feedback.

Jim Trerise, my co-manager, who assumed enormous responsibilities and additional work so I could embark on this road to learning.

My family and friends, Jennifer, Guy, Brad, and Michelle for encouraging me and having the confidence I could succeed.

My husband, Odd, for your support, kindness, patience, and understanding. Thank you for the many, many romantic dinners at fine restaurants, where we discussed and read my thesis.

Success is not mine alone—it is shared with each of you.

CHAPTER ONE: FOCUS AND FRAMING

The focus of my research study is the Rotary Club of Prince Rupert, chartered in 1921, and currently has 58 members. Rotary Club membership represents a cross-section of local business, professional, and community-minded people, who participate in fellowship, service, and fund-raising activities. Its membership comprises of volunteers who choose to give freely of their time, energy, and talents to help other people and do so without expectation of compensation. "Volunteering time for a variety of purposes or caring and sharing has been a part of most societies throughout human history" (Hodgkinson, 2003, p. 35).

Rotary members dedicate their time, skills, expertise, and myriad other resources toward improving human conditions. Belonging to Rotary gives men and women an opportunity to contribute to their local and global communities, as well as personal enjoyment and social well-being, through participation and fellowship with other members. To further understand the Rotary Club as a volunteer organization and the service to the community, it was necessary to discuss the overview of Rotary and the significance of the opportunity.

Overview of Rotary

The Rotary Club is a member of the global system of Rotary International, which provides members the opportunity to participate in worldwide activities. Rotary International was founded in 1905 and has a rich heritage of public service throughout the world. Today, nearly 1.2 million members from more that 32,000 Rotary Clubs in 200 countries serve as volunteers in their local, district, and world communities (Rotary International, 2007d, ¶ 1-2). Rotarians initiate local community and international projects that address many of today's most critical issues, such as violence, drug abuse, contaminated drinking water, hunger, illiteracy, polio, AIDS, and the environment (Rotary International, 2007c, ¶ 12). The organization also supports programs for youth, educational opportunities, and international exchange for career development (Rotary International, 2007h, ¶ 3). Rotary provides opportunities for its members to participate in a wide variety of projects and programs, and it is imperative that their efforts, dedication of time, and expertise, both to raise funds and provide services, are placed to best meet the needs of their community. Therefore, it was appropriate that my research question asked how the Rotary Club of Prince Rupert (Rotary Club) can best expand its volunteer service to its community.

As well as serving the community, the Rotary Club has activities for the members such as weekly lunch meetings and fellowship. This gives the members the opportunity to hear interesting speakers, receive club updates from the directors and member reports on various club projects, and to plan service activities. These clubs are autonomous and determine their own service projects, based on both local needs and international projects. Rotary Clubs are non religious, nongovernmental (Rotary International, 2007d, ¶ 2), and open to every race and culture, welcoming everyone as equals (Eliasoph, 2003, p. 205). Rotary International exemplifies what Rotary is and Rotary does, as stated more than 30 years ago by the Past Rotary International President:

> We cannot possibly administer an organization with the ramifications of Rotary International, or even a Rotary Club, without mechanics, techniques, and procedures. If, then, we

3

are to have such machinery, let us have the best possible. But it is important to know and remember that the machinery is not an end in itself—it is a means to an end. The objective is better Rotary, and better Rotarians (Thomas, 1974, p. 56).

Also, as members of Rotary International, these local club members contribute their time and expertise to provide the commendable work that they do. The Rotary Club also donates annually to The Rotary Foundation for international service and education, particularly in the developing world.

In contrast to the wonderful work of members to raise these funds, I have seen the challenges within the Rotary Club in the declining membership and limited participation by members in club activities. I have been involved in most facets of the Rotary Club. In 2004, Rotary International's centennial year, I was elected the first woman President of the Rotary Club, after serving in many capacities as chair of various committees, as well as five years as secretary and a term as treasurer.

From these various positions, I have been able to observe many of the attributes, as well as the problems, inherent in volunteer organizations. This research and application of findings have formed the basis for my research inquiry. Hence, through a process known as community-based action research, I had explored and identified strategies for strengthening the volunteer base, so the club can meet the needs of the members while serving the community.

The aim of my research was succinctly stated by Stringer (1999) as "not to establish the truth or to describe what really is happening, but to reveal the different truths and realities—constructions—held by different individuals and groups" within the community (p. 45). This research identified the means to build collaboration that enabled the members and the community to formulate mutually acceptable solutions for everyone's benefit (p. 188). As a result, I established the following research question and subquestions.

My research question was: How can the Rotary Club of Prince Rupert best expand its volunteer service to its community? Subquestions included:

1. What are the expectations by the community of the Rotary Club of Prince Rupert?

2. How has the club currently met the members' needs in order to retain and strengthen the membership?

3. What have the members done to make the Rotary Club of Prince Rupert a stronger volunteer community organization so that the Rotary Club of Prince Rupert can better serve the community?

The Opportunity

The opportunities for the Rotary Club are endless. Kouzes and Posner (2002) suggested, "Leaders inspire a shared vision, in which the people imagine an exciting, highly attractive future for their organization—visions and dreams of what could be" (p. 15). Leaders have the belief they are confident in their abilities to make extraordinary things happen. Kouzes and Posner further described that "every organization begins with a dream, which is the force that invents the future" (p. 15).

To develop that dream, the Rotary Club needs to plan for the future, and my research project was a timely opportunity to seek new challenges, create new vision, and seriously get involved in the leading edge. It is time to let go of the belief that this is the way it has always been done and the often-heard comment that, if it works, why fix it?

However, equally important to remember is that the future is built upon the past. The chances are that the "resources that move the organization forward will be largely drawn from the same resources that brought it to where it is today" (Bellman, 1990, p. 74).

It was my belief that learning from one another—members who have years of experience, combined with new members' energy and new ideas—was a very powerful combination and must be communicated in a way that does not threaten and is welcoming and approachable. Groups with a common purpose and vision, such as Rotary, "create the conditions that will mobilize their energy, engage their enthusiasm, and generate activity that can be productively applied to the resolution of issues and problems that concern them" (Stringer, 1999, p. 28). For these various reasons, my research used community-based action research, which involved both the community and Rotary Club members, to identify areas of mutual interests, goals, and objectives for themselves and for the Rotary Club.

It was appropriate and opportune that the President of Rotary International challenged local clubs to strengthen their organization, through being more attractive to potential new members and retaining the members they have for their Rotary Clubs, to be able to better meet the needs of the communities they serve. "Stronger clubs make it far more likely that your clubs will attract the kinds of members you want as your fellow Rotarians" (W. Boyd, personal communication, January 22, 2007).

This challenge to its members was meant to motivate the local club to seek new ways to make Rotary stronger, thereby making our communities better. To make the club better, we must ensure we have ample members to provide the services required. This is a wonderful opportunity to find ways to entice more people to join Rotary and seek opportunities for our club to grow stronger and more attractive, so that we can expand volunteer services in the community.

Significance of the Opportunity

In these economically challenging times, the Rotary Club needs to identify other creative and innovative ways to raise funds, to continue with its financial assistance to organizations in services or projects that benefit the community. Prince Rupert has seen a substantial decline in its population since the Skeena Cellulose Ltd. closed its pulp mill in June

2001 (Prince Rupert Economic Department, personal communication, October 19, 2007). The pulp mill employed approximately 700 workers and with its closure has caused an estimated 350 families to move away to find employment elsewhere. As well as the closure of the pulp mill, the fishing industry was in decline. When fishing was at its peak operations, it is believed that the industry employed around 2,825 fishers and cannery workers. In contrast, today, it is estimated that there are only 1,515 fishers and cannery workers (O. Eidsvik, personal communication, July 20, 2007). As a result, the population of Prince Rupert declined from 16,714 people in 1996 to 12,815 people in 2006 (BC Stats, 2007). Therefore, with the population decline, the membership of the Rotary Club has decreased as well, which has placed the club in a state of change.

When we are faced with new challenges, we live with a high degree of ambiguity. "Change and the accompanying uncertainty throw us off our equilibrium. Yet, it is these fluctuations, disturbances, and imbalances in organizations that are the primary sources of creativity" (Kouzes & Posner, 2002, p. 186). To build on this creativity, the Rotary Club must search for opportunities by seeking innovative ways to change and grow. The exciting new changes will result in the rejuvenation of the members, by giving them new and different challenges.

The Rotary Club needs to change the way it thinks, offers challenges, and ultimately changes, so the members will be committed and enrolled. "Enrolment is a natural process from genuine enthusiasm for a vision and willingness to let others come to their own choice" (Senge, 2006, p. 206). Therefore, as leaders of the Rotary Club, it is your duty to entice your members to be enrolled to achieve commitment and satisfaction, by identifying and seizing the opportunities to become a stronger volunteer organization. Conversely, the Rotary Club needs to be cognizant of what will happen to the organization, if the members do not address this opportunity for growth and change.

It is important members of the Rotary Club realize that, without growth and change, the result could be loss of members, due to members not being challenged by new activities. Members may become stagnant by merely attending meetings because they are required to do so. As a result, the club can lose the vibrancy of an active, happy, and satisfied membership that is evident today.

It is imperative that the club prepare a strategy to develop a stronger club, to enable its members to meet the service expectations of our community, as well as giving those challenges and satisfaction to the members in their volunteer service. It is the hope that my research project will give the Rotary Club that strategic planning process to achieve member retention so it has enough members to perform its services. It is an important time for the leaders of the Rotary Club to strategically plan for the future of the organization.

Therefore, in the planning for the future, the significance of the opportunity for the Rotary Club is that this research project can form the basis of the strategic plan that will take it into the next decade of service to the community. As well as the benefits to the Rotary Club, the significance of the opportunity also challenged me into finding the answers through research and inquiry, rather than instinct and past experience. My leadership stretch was in using tools of research and applying the findings to real situations. As well, to accomplish this research study, it was necessary to review the system analysis of the opportunity to understand how the Rotary Club related within the global system of Rotary International.

System Analysis of the Opportunity

The application of these situations to real situations required me to describe the entire system that would impact the opportunity. The system includes the organization within the global, cultural, and societal components in which the project has taken place. The following will describe the factors and underlying issues that influence the opportunities.

> The Object of Rotary is to encourage and foster the ideal of service as a basis of worthy enterprise and, in particular, to encourage and foster: FIRST. The development of acquaintance as an opportunity for service; SECOND. High ethical standards in business and professions, the recognition of the worthiness of all useful occupations, and the dignifying of each Rotarian's occupation as an opportunity to serve society; THIRD. The application of the ideal of service in each Rotarian's personal, business, and community life; and, FOURTH. The advancement of international understanding, goodwill, and peace through a world fellowship of business and professional persons united in the ideal of service (Rotary International, 2007a, ¶ 1–5).

In an era of globalization and democratization, volunteering is rapidly being recognized as the entity that helps hold societies together and as an additional useful resource in solving social community problems (Hodgkinson, 2003, p. 36). In the global system, Rotary

International is the parent organization to which all Rotary Clubs must belong.

Within Rotary International are 530 districts whose role is to be the liaison between the local clubs and Rotary International and to assist their member clubs in all matters pertaining to Rotary (Rotary International, 2007g, ¶ 2). The other primary function of the District, as stated in the District Manual, is club member development and training through regional seminars and district conferences (Rotary International District 5040, 2007b, p. 62). The value of training sessions is the vast learning for all members, not only for the volunteer aspects, but for their professional and social development of skills. Rotary District 5040 is comprised of 2,100 Rotarians in 56 clubs encompassing most of British Columbia (see Figure 1), but not including Fort St. John, Okanagan, or Kootenay areas (p. 74). This provides the opportunity for access to many clubs, members and resources throughout the district.

It is imperative that Rotary Clubs collectively realize that, as stated by Bussell and Forbes (2001), "It is the members who bring the new fresh ideas, either from their own experiences and skills or from those with whom they are in contact" (p. 244). Rotarians are active community members and, therefore, are valuable sources of input and information. People also endeavour to work in harmony within their membership, through identifying shared problems and collaborating to find solutions that benefit themselves, as well as the organization (Wheatley, 1999, p. 70).

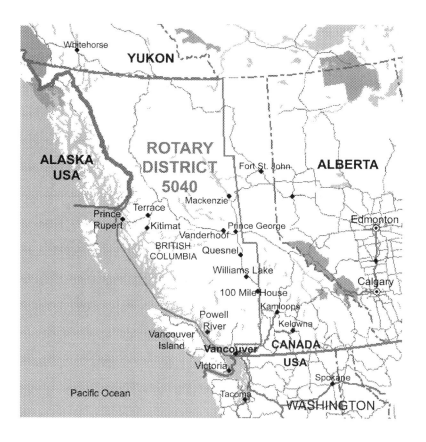

Figure 1. Map of District 5040

At the beginning of my research, I was not aware of significant organizational politics or variables that were evident within the membership. However, as I proceeded with the research, organizational decisions that could affect the outcomes of the current context and priorities became evident. As my leadership stretch mentioned previously was my reliance on experience and intuitions, I intentionally did not identify these issues prior to the commencement of the project or during the process and left it to the research to identify these matters of organizational politics. As a result, it was necessary to understand the organizational content of the Rotary Club.

Organizational Content

The Rotary Club of Prince Rupert is a legally constituted body incorporated 85 years ago. The Board is comprised of the President, President-elect, Past President, Secretary, Treasurer, and 6 directors for a total of 11 members. The President-elect is automatically declared

President, and a new President-elect is elected. There are three directors who are elected for a two-year term, and three directors will serve their last-year term for purposes of continuity. The Secretary and Treasurer are elected for a one-year term, but can serve additional years upon being re-elected. The Rotary Club is mandated to elect its officers annually at its Annual General Meeting held each year prior to December 31, and the term of office is from July 1 to June 30 of each year. Although the administration of the Rotary Club is under the general supervision of Rotary International, each Rotary Club has its own constitution and by-laws (Rotary Club of Prince Rupert, 2006).

Rotary International has identified specific areas of service for its member Rotary Clubs and has provided the *Club Leadership Plan* (Rotary International, Leadership Education and Training Division, 2005; see Figure 2), which all Rotary Clubs are encouraged to support and include in their club directives. The Four Avenues of Service are the Club Service, Vocational Service, Community Service, and International Service (p. 10).

There is great value in an organization that establishes a Board of Directors and committees that are made up of a diverse collection of individuals, who have different behaviour patterns, diverse opinions, and a world of experiences (Leblanc & Gillies, 2005, p. 140). People with a high level of personal mastery have a special sense of purpose that lies behind their visions and goals. They see "reality as an ally, not an enemy" (Senge, 2006, p. 132).

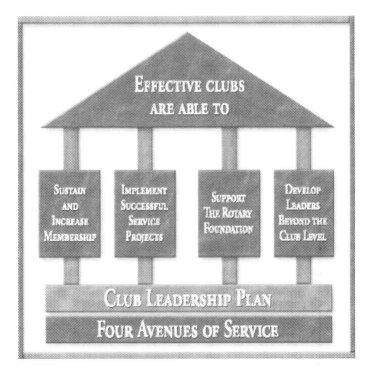

Figure 2. Rotary International club leadership plan.

Note: From *Club Leadership Plan* (p. 1) by Rotary International, Leadership Education and Training Division, 2005, Evanston, IL: Rotary International. Copyright 2005 by Rotary International. Reprinted with permission.

A true value of an organization is that everyone has their own unique talents, expertise, and knowledge. It is the combination of all these qualities that make the organization a vast culmination of abilities. As Quinn (2004) stated, "Everyone comes with a unique gifts, we are as different as snowflakes, but to realize and use these gifts we have to use our courage and move forward with a commitment to true service" (p. 17). In similar words, DePree (2003) stated, "Everyone comes with certain gifts—but not the same gifts" (p. 26).

"The power in organizations is the capacity generated by relationships" (Wheatley, 1999, p. 39) and people knowing how to listen and speak to each other. "There is obvious evidence of trust and respect" (p. 39). The literature review confirmed that our best knowledge already exists within our own organization. The strategy is to accomplish the organizational goals and how to apply this knowledge for maximum benefit.

Organizations need volunteers to exist and to achieve its goals and objectives. According to the report by Independent Sector and United Nations Volunteers (Dingle, 2000), there are three criteria for volunteering: "(a) it is not primarily for financial gain, (b) it is of one's own free will, and (c) it brings benefits to a third party as well as to the people who volunteer" (pp. 9–10). Rotary members meet these three criteria for volunteering, because they believe in giving mutual aid to those in need and service to others. As a result, it is evident volunteer organizations have become the "chief way for thousands of people to focus individual efforts into truly marvellous achievements" (DePree, 2003, p. 34).

Unfortunately, the decline in volunteering is impacting all service clubs and is a serious concern for the Rotary organization. It is imperative for Rotary Clubs to recognize that member retention is equally important as obtaining new members. One way to ensure that members are retained is by meeting the reasons why the member joined Rotary and, thereby, providing quality community service. Every person has his or her own specific reason for becoming involved. Therefore, it is imperative that the leaders within the Rotary Club become aware of what each member wants from their membership with the club or what gives them satisfaction. It is important that the "individual's motivation to volunteering does not end with his or her recruitment" (Clary & Snyder, 1999, p. 156). Without this knowledge, the Rotary

Club may not be meeting the needs of its own members and, thereby, losing their membership.

Therefore, to obtain this knowledge of member needs and wants, the main external influence on the opportunity of my research was the community itself, as my question included evaluation of Rotary's volunteer service to the community. The Rotary Club is very fortunate that other community organizations in Prince Rupert are supportive of the Rotary Club, and many of these organizations have members in the Rotary Club.

Public Awareness of Rotary

However, the people of Prince Rupert appeared to lack knowledge about Rotary and what Rotary does, which had influence on the opportunities that this research project addressed (Eli, 2006). Francis Eli, a student in Business Administration at the North West Community College in Prince Rupert, prepared an analysis of the knowledge level of Rotary within the community. Her conclusion was that public awareness needs to be addressed. She stated that the Rotary Club is losing recognition with the public and should take measures to provide information of what Rotary does and gives to the community. Ms. Eli's report was presented to the Rotary membership in December 2006.

To accomplish this public awareness program, the Rotary Club must ensure that its members act as ambassadors to the community, and the club is seen by the public as a service organization that dedicates countless volunteer hours, skills, and resources to improving human conditions locally and globally. Therefore, to assist the Rotary Club to reach its potential for volunteer services, it was an opportune time for my research project to challenge the members to become enrolled and committed to seizing the opportunities to become a stronger and visible volunteer organization. Conversely, the Rotary Club needs to be cognizant that, if members do not address this opportunity for growth and change, the result could be stagnation, lack of vibrancy, and bored members who will soon leave the organization to seek other challenges.

This opportunity for growth and change will be the force that initiates the Rotary Club to develop a strategic plan as recommended by the Rotary International *Club Leadership Plan* (Rotary International, Leadership Education and Training Division, 2005). This strategic plan will be the roadmap to the future vision and goals of the Rotary Club. It is therefore, imperative to this study, to review what the academic writers have said about volunteer organizations, their leadership, the volunteers and the community. It is the endeavour of the literature review to identify the process of change so my research can determine how the Rotary Club of Prince Rupert ca best expand its volunteer services to the meet the needs of the community.

CHAPTER TWO: LITERATURE REVIEW

A literature review is used to look at what other academic writers and researchers have "done in areas that are similar, though not necessarily identical, to one's own area of investigation" (Leedy & Ormrod, 2005, p. 64). This literature reviewed my research question, "How can the Rotary Club of Prince Rupert best expand its volunteer service to the community?" and explored the relevant three concepts which were: (a) overview of volunteer organizations, (b) the volunteers, and (c) the community. In order to identify and address these issues and my research question, I researched what academic authors have said about each of my concepts and used their literature to guide me in the approach of my research project.

Overview of Volunteer Organizations

The overview of the volunteer organizations studies the reasons volunteer organizations exist, the value of such organizations, and their leadership. Wolf (1999) stated volunteer organizations "give the volunteer their own sense of place and allow them a chance to advance within the volunteer structure" (p. 105). Inglehart (2003) believed the causes for which people volunteer are: (a) environmental; (b) political; and (c) services that include religious, youth, sports, professional, and cultural groups (p. 63). This definition would include the Rotary Club as an example of a service organization that gives its members a sense of belonging and the opportunity to provide volunteer services to its community, because the volunteer organizations are about the people they serve. Therefore, it is necessary to study the literature on volunteer organizations, successful volunteer organizations, the volunteer organizations as a system, and the leadership of volunteer organizations.

Volunteer Organizations

Volunteer organizations exist because they care about the people they serve (DePree, 2003, p. 91). It is this genuine caring and the creating of an organization that will better serve all the people of the communities and those who volunteer (Bellman, 2002, p. 161). One of the greatest values of organizations such as Rotary is the caring for others, as stated by both DePree and Bellman. This caring is evidenced by the "way people in an organization treat each other is possibly the single most influential factor in determining the success or failure of an organization in change" (Gann, 1996, p. 40). As Rotarians, our conduct is influenced by the motto of Rotary International (2007f): "Service Above Self" (¶ 1). Through this mandate, Rotarians ensure these values established by Rotary International are respected, honoured, and consistently practiced.

"The impact of these values, vision, and culture occupies a great deal of organizational attention. We see their effects on organizational vitality, even if we cannot define why they are such potent forces" (Wheatley, 1999, p. 14). For example, Rotary has established a conduct of values and ethical statement called the Four-Way Test (Rotary International, 2007a) by which each Rotarian is required to measure his or her life accordingly. "Of the things we think, say or do (1) is it the truth, (2) is it fair to all concerned, (3) does it build goodwill and better friendships, [and] (4) will it be beneficial to all concerned?" (¶ 11-12).

As Rotarians, we should have the Four-Way Test in mind in every decision we make, all day long. Our utmost responsibility is to speak the truth, to be fair, to build goodwill and better friendships, and to do our very best in all situations (¶ 10).

Organizations are "where people continually expand their capacity to create the results they truly desire, where new and expansive patterns of thinking are nurtured, where collective aspirations are set free, and where people are continually learning how to learn together" (Senge, 2006, p. 3). When these attributes and aspirations of the volunteer are nurtured, the result is a successful volunteer organization.

Successful Volunteer Organizations

Successful volunteer organizations are well organized to meet the needs of the volunteers and are sensitive to the needs of those involved. To accomplish this, the organization must have a clear vision and goals that are communicated and readily accessible to its members. Volunteer organizations give people the opportunity to bring their "diverse talents, perspectives, and constituencies together to form an integrated, dynamic whole" (Bennis & Goldsmith, 2003, p. 6).

These "volunteer organizations give people the opportunity to satisfy their need to put something back to the community that has given them so much" (Gann, 1996, p. 101). Individual people want to share and contribute their services and benefits with the people within their communities. By doing so through organizations, they can collectively make a greater impact than one person working on his or her own. Wheatley (1999) very effectively summarized these actions that, because our existence, are within a system: "We never know how our small activities will affect others through the invisible fabric of our connectedness" (p. 45).

It is this service and the positive impact upon the volunteer that makes a successful service organization of today. It is the ability of the volunteer and organization to be able to provide people with what they need. Gann (1996) stated volunteer organizations are not different in their functions from any other managed structures (private sector) with a purpose and their mandate is "to provide what people need at the best quality and at a manageable cost" (p. 2). While source of funding of the private sector and accountability is different, the justification of voluntary organizations is much the same (p. 2). Although it is necessary to consider Gann's comparisons of the similarities between volunteer organizations and for-profit organizations, it is equally important to be cognizant of the differences. Volunteer organizations do differ from the private enterprises, as most have the mandate to be not-for-profit and obtain operating funds from member dues, community donations, and fundraising. This is different than the private sector organization whose mandate must be for profit. The two are similar. As stated by Gann, volunteer organizations are value driven and have unique abilities to collect and disseminate information in a way that is "quite free of political or commercial consideration" (p. 4).

> Rotary International stated, now more than ever, we need a vision and knowledge of what is happening around us, a new view of cultural and religious phenomena, without dividing humankind into limited and subjective categories. That's the tenet for a better world and a job for us Rotarians: not engaging in politics, but serving without any boundaries (Fredricksson, 2007, ¶ 12).

However, in contrast, Eliasoph (2003) believed that "volunteer associations teach citizens to care about each other and yet the same association can also teach them not to care about politics" (p. 200). Eliasoph stated that speaking about politics "gives political concern meaning and form, providing socially recognizable tools for thinking and acting. Volunteers find ample reasons to avoid talking politics in voluntary associations" (p. 200). Eliasoph further substantiated the value of talking politics: "You really can make a difference on issues that are close to home" (p. 200).

To be a successful volunteer organization and because of the sensitive nature of cultural, political, and religion affiliations, Rotary International must meet the needs of the volunteers and be sensitive to the needs of those involved. Therefore, as a world-wide organization, it is necessary for Rotary International to study the influence of the volunteer organization as a system.

Volunteer Organizations as a System

The ability for the Rotary Club to participate in the variety of services to the community is seen as a result of their being part of a larger system. Each Rotary Club belongs to Rotary International. Rotary International is the parent organization that has nearly 1.2 million members from more that 32,000 Rotary Clubs in 200 countries (Rotary International, 2007d, ¶ 1–2). As part of a system, it gives organizations the opportunity to serve their community by using their talents to provide goods and services (Bellman, 2002, p. 160).

Bellman (2002) identified concerns with organizations becoming too large, as "large organizations are awkward and unwieldy and as a result do not work very well because they cannot relate to the people who work in them" (p. 161). He saw large organizations as becoming more mechanical by not creating rich, life-filled, working entities. He claimed that "organizations are being modeled after machines—mechanical, repetitious, predictable, and inflexible" (p. 161). To alleviate these concerns, Rotary International has a Board of Directors as the administrative body of Rotary International, with 19 members including the Rotary International President, President-elect, and 17 directors who are nominated by the clubs and elected at the Rotary International Convention representing various districts from throughout the world. The Rotary International Board controls and manages Rotary International affairs and funds in conformity with the Rotary International Constitution and Bylaws. For continuity, each director serves a term of two years (Rotary International, ¶ 1).

Rotary International with members throughout the world is greatly affected by occurrences in any country. Wheatley (1999) observed that the "fall of the Berlin Wall demonstrated the power of 'think globally, act locally.' It proves that local actions can have enormous influence on a monstrous system that has resisted all other political attempts to change it" (p. 44). Since Rotary is an international organization, the growth of members globally adds to the overall membership of Rotary. Membership for both Rotary International and its member clubs are greatly influenced by the leadership of their organizations. It is, therefore, the intent of this study to review the impact of leadership on volunteer organizations.

Leadership of Volunteer Organizations

Leadership of volunteer organizations need to know the reasons why people volunteer and what keeps them committed to the organization. However, leadership within Rotary Clubs presents difficult challenges, because their membership is a collage of adult learning issues incorporating a variety of generational personalities and cultural differences. A good leader must be cognizant of how best to lead such a diverse group of individuals. The leader must be able to relate to the volunteers' way of communication, learning, and need to achieve desired outcomes from their participation in the organization. In this section of the literature review, I looked at the importance of leaders understanding adult learning, appreciating the generational differences among those they are leading, and understanding cultural differences among those being led, as it is the leadership that will influence the success of that volunteer organization.

> Good leaders make people feel that they are at the heart of things, not at the periphery. Everyone feels that he/she makes a difference to the success of the organization. When that happens, people feel centered and that gives their work meaning (Bennis & Goldsmith, 2003, p. 5).

Challenges of Leadership

Bennis and Goldsmith's (2003) comments confirm how important it is to be aware of how to influence the success of the organization. One specific strategy is to know that adult learning issues are very complex and individual to each person. Therefore, the leader needs to know how adults react to new experiences and certain situations. Each adult has different learning styles and may hear the same information, but each may derive a very different interpretation of that information (MacKeracher, 2006, pp. 78–80). Adults also react differently to the same situations. Some adults like to proceed with activities by learning more about the issue and constant questioning; others may begin by setting goals and be process oriented, while others just want to get going without further thought (p. 87).

Knowing the different ways in which adults learn, a good leader must also be cognizant that adults can feel threatened by trying new and different things and may be hesitant about participating or becoming involved. This feeling, by the adult, of being threatened is due to adults' self-concepts being already well organized and their feeling that they "stand to lose much of their previous gains in self-esteem and self-confidence" (MacKeracher, 2006, p. 126). "[For] adults to become fully engaged in learning, they must be aroused, feel relatively safe, and be willing and able to channel their motives into the learning process" (p. 127). Adults, to learn and participate, need a supportive and encouraging environment that does not threaten them.

To add to the adult learning issues, generational differences are very evident and prominent within the total membership of the Rotary

Club, and different generations have very different needs and wants. Rotary membership encompasses each of the generations ranging from the veterans who were born before World War II, the Baby Boomers born between 1945 and 1963, the generation Xers born between 1964 and 1979, and the most recent group of generation Nexters born after 1980 (Durkin, 2007, ¶ 5). Each generation views life very differently, has varying attitudes and diverse talents, and understands life in its own unique way.

The veterans, or seniors, are ages 60 and up, and their values were shaped by the Great Depression, two World Wars, and the Korean War. As a result of these experiences, their values emphasize civic pride, loyalty, and respect for authority, dedication, sacrifice, conformity, home, and discipline (Durkin, 2007, ¶ 6–7). The next generation, called Baby Boomers, grew up during the Vietnam War, Woodstock, civil rights movement, and the beginning of the space era with the landing on the moon (¶ 8–9). These experiences shaped their values of extreme optimism, opportunity and progress, loyalty, being team players, and their need for acceptance from others (Hamlin, 2006, p. 8).

Following the Baby Boomers come the generation Xers, who came of age during the economic wars of the 1970s and 1980s. Their values were shaped by the Watergate scandal, which brought about the impeachment of the President of the United States, the Space Shuttle Challenger disaster, terrorism, and computers. Often left to fend for themselves by working parents, they spent their time surfing the Web, playing video games, and watching TV. In the process, "they developed a chronic need for stimulation and instant gratification" (Durkin, ¶ 10–11). They projected the attitude that anything goes; they are "outspoken, mobile, desire the good life and generally give the appearance of being lazy and uncaring" (Hamlin, 2006, p. 28).

The final group is the Generation Y, sometimes called Nexters. Raised in a high-tech world that shaped their entire value system, many of them became truly global, spoke several languages, are well traveled, and as a result, have a tendency to be very outspoken. In contrast with the earlier generations whose preference is to read written text, this generation of young people do not read text in print, as they "depend mostly on the computer, cell phones, and text messaging" (Hamlin, 2006, p. 35).

One can readily see the challenges of combining all these generations as members into one organization, such as Rotary: (a) the older members, who are set in the ways they have always done things and not willing to take risks; (b) the baby boomers, who just need to be liked and included; (c) the Xers, who do not wait for information, consumed with their computers and TV; and (d) the Yers or Nexters, who think they know it all, with a make-it-up-as-you-go attitude and a strong resistance to the established system. The generational differences make it difficult for everyone to be excited about the same things. Hamlin (2006) stated, "Generation goals, needs, beliefs and priorities are the key to reaching and motivating each generational group" (p. 41). Rotary leaders have many challenges, as the organization is made up of adults with a conglomeration of generational differences.

Another issue posing a great challenge to the leadership of volunteer organizations is the cultural differences of members, who are influenced by different cultures, ethnic beliefs, and religious influences. These multicultural groups who live in our communities have brought with them their ethnic roots, their culture and religious observations, and their wish to hold on to their national identity. They also bring with them their own languages and beliefs that affect their attitudes and actions. The way to communicate with people of different generations, background, and ethnicity is to make them feel comfortable, anticipate their needs, encourage dialogue, and use verbal language that is clear and easy to understand (Hamlin, 2006, p. 46).

Therefore, these numerous challenges of personal goals, generation influences, and cultural beliefs require a leader to possess the variety of skills and abilities to ensure the diverse group of volunteers understand their roles and responsibilities. To address the issue of leader roles and responsibilities, many books have incorporated these rules and responsibilities into various manuals or board rule books (Wolf, 1999, p. 51). Carver (2002) developed a model of governance called "Policy Governance" (p. 580). Differing with Wolf's and Carver's views, Secretan (1997) suggested that "excessive structure creates negative energy blocks preventing the free flow of positive energy" (p. 170). He believed that the role of every leader was to inspire those he was leading. Senge (2006) combined both views and stated, "Continually finding the right balance between too much and too little structure, will be a key to having the adaptive capabilities to survive" (p. 276).

Volunteers must have defined roles and responsibilities to give the organization structure. However, within the parameters of roles and responsibilities, it is important to consider Secretan's (1997) belief that creative and unstructured definition of free thinking and unencumbered participation can be effective and rewarding for the volunteers of the Rotary Clubs.

Leadership Motivating Volunteers

Along with inspiring others, it is also an important factor for leaders to know how and when to motivate the volunteers—especially when pay and benefits are not incentives (Tretter & Tuttle, 2005, p. 8). Because volunteers are not paid, Secretan (1997) contended that there needs to be a reward system that "specifically meets the intrinsic as well as the extrinsic needs of each individual" (p. 127). One known method of inspiring and motivating volunteers is to recognize the volunteers' need to be involved in decision-making, implementation of plans, and share in mutual participation within the organization (Riggio & Orr,

2004, p. 164). Rotary members who are involved on committees are given the opportunities to participate in decision-making. As these members become more involved and participate in Rotary training programmes, they are soon considered for leadership roles within the club.

Organizations that drift away from fully-participating models soon find that volunteers have a tendency to become upset and feel that the organization has lost its direction and sense of purpose. Leaders of volunteers need to be responsive to volunteer needs and opinions to keep them committed and active (Riggio & Orr, 2004, p. 164). In the absence of monetary rewards, leaders must be especially concerned with the social and psychological benefits volunteers receive as a result of their service work. Volunteers who receive something back from their work are more likely to stay involved.

To ensure that leaders recognize that volunteers need to achieve satisfaction in their volunteer work as a way of getting something back from their involvement, the leader must also realize "that leadership techniques that are successful in the corporate world do not always work in the volunteer world" (Tretter & Tuttle, 2005, p. 7), because salaries and bonus incentives do not exist for the volunteers. As the success or failure of the mission and goals of an organization, whether volunteer or corporate, is dependent upon leadership, the leaders must be aware of the influence they have on the volunteers and volunteer organizations and ensure the volunteers' desires for involvement and the attainments of their personal goals are met. One can readily see the difficulties for leaders when there are so many aspects that influence the various views and opinions of the membership. An effective leader will ensure that everyone is included and acknowledges that each person does make a difference by their contributions to the success of the organization. Leadership of volunteer organizations need to know the reasons why people volunteer and what keeps them committed to the organization. A good leader needs to be cognizant of how best to lead such a diverse group of individuals. The leader must be able to relate to the volunteers' way of communication, learning, and need to achieve desired outcomes from their participation in the organization. Therefore, it is important for leaders to understand volunteer, what keeps the volunteer committed to the organization, and what the volunteer needs and wants form that organization.

The Volunteer

To ensure that volunteers remain committed to the organization, each person must be given the opportunity to contribute to the organization. It is important to know the reasons a person volunteers, as Rotary membership retention is dependent upon meeting the needs and reasons why a person becomes a member. Therefore, membership retention is a major concern of Rotary. It is important to recognize that volunteers want to make a contribution to their organization and to live with purpose by giving of themselves to a worthy cause (Hybels, 2004, p. 35). Therefore, it is important to both (a) understand the reasons why people volunteer and (b) to retain and attract members, as volunteer trends indicate a decline in people volunteering.

Often, the reason volunteers become involved is the personal growth and experience. Ladd (1999) has found that a valuable benefit to the volunteer is training in citizenship skills; whereby, the volunteer becomes a better person through learning to share and help others (p. 61). Kouzes and Posner (2002) stated volunteers must "make a statement with your life that is consistent with your heart, that gives voice to what you really feel is really important" (p. 54), and whatever you decide to do, do so by being true to whom you are.

Another reason people volunteer is to do what is true to who they are and want. Hybels (2004) had discovered that when volunteers were all working harder than they ever imagined, they realized they were having a great deal of fun in the process (p. 44). This enjoyment of volunteer activities is the fellowship found in Rotary and is one of the primary objectives of the organization. In doing projects, members also discovered they were learning skills they did not know they had and were being given additional opportunities to learn.

It is important to realize and recognize that volunteers participate for many reasons. The successful organization recognizes the variety of reasons that volunteers join their organization, thereby retaining the members they have, while attracting others to join.

Reasons to Volunteer

There are a variety of reasons volunteers want to get involved. For some volunteers, it is the opportunity to learn and improve oneself. In Rotary, it has been discovered that some volunteers enjoy serving in a way that is very different from what they do in their work. Volunteers seek to serve outside their areas of professional expertise. It is equally important to realize that some people find satisfaction in serving in what they do best, as in their lifelong work. Hybels (2004) has also discovered this in his relationships with volunteer organizations (p. 86).

DePree (2003) astutely stated, "Everyone comes with a certain gift—but not all with the same gifts" (p. 26). It is these diverse talents and abilities that make volunteers from all walks of life so valuable in their contributions to the community.

Membership has its challenges of culturally-diverse people from various generations, ranging from the early adults to retired senior citizens. Gann (1996) cautioned that leaders must to be cognizant to ensure that older members do not protect their position by not passing on information to the newer members (p. 96). Gann further stated,

> As new members are recruited and original members become protective of their own vision and can be perceived by new members as a sense of superiority over them. These feelings can get in the way of development and growth of the club, by making new member feel intrusive, especially when they hear older members saying, "Wasn't it great when . . . ?" (p. 95)

There is serious need to be cognizant of this change within an organization, especially when new members are actively being sought to increase membership primarily during a period when volunteer trends indicate a decline in participation.

Declining Volunteer Trends

Membership retention and recruitment are major focuses for the Rotary Club, and Rotary International is extremely concerned with the membership decline within some clubs in the western world. However, positive growth is seen in other parts of the world. Rotary International (2007e, ¶ 12) reported that, following the collapse of the Berlin Wall and the dissolution of the Soviet Union, Rotary Clubs were formed or re-established throughout Central and Eastern Europe, thus adding greatly to the total membership within Rotary (History section, ¶ 12).

The Canadian 2000 National Survey of Giving, Volunteering, and Participating (Statistics Canada, 2001) showed that, in the previous year, 6.5 million Canadians, or 27% of the population aged 15 and older, volunteered through an organization. This is a decline from the

7.5 million or 31% of the population who volunteered in 1997. There were fewer volunteers in 2000 despite there being more Canadians; the population of Canada increased by almost 2.5% from 1997 to 2000 (p. 9).

I have not recorded the recently-dated *2004 National Survey of Giving, Volunteering and Participating* (NSGVP) statistics (Statistics Canada, 2005), as this report stated there was a phenomenal increase in the 2003 volunteering, which reached 11.8 million Canadians, or 45% of the population volunteered. The 2004 NSGVP acknowledged it has recorded a large increase in volunteering. There may be evidence to support the direction of the increased volunteer trend; however, changes in questionnaire content and collection methodology, coupled with a relatively low response rate, and a changing awareness in the Canadian population of the importance of volunteering, may have contributed to the magnitude of the trend (p. 74). The reader is cautioned that the 2004 statistics may not be reliable for the purpose of this research.

Trends have indicated there is a decline of volunteers and volunteer organizations over the past several years (Putnam, 2000; Statistics Canada, 2001). Therefore, it is important that the Rotary Club recognizes the impact of this decline and endeavours to continue to be a volunteer organization that offers their members the opportunity to meet the reasons for which they joined Rotary.

It is also imperative for leaders to be aware of what negatively affects volunteers. Hybels (2004) described some willing-hearted volunteers as having been wounded while volunteering. Too often, this happens to volunteers who respond to an invitation to serve, only to end up with an experience that was "poorly conceived, resulting in tasks that few people would find fulfilling" (p. 25). We have all found ourselves in that position, when we show up to serve and discover there is nothing to do. This type of occurrence causes volunteers to lose precious hours they had willingly set aside in their busy schedule. The easiest way to lose a volunteer is to waste his or her valuable time (p. 115).

Drucker (1990) reiterated this experience, as most people do not volunteer for an organization if they do not share the vision of that organization (p. 189). Volunteers who do not get satisfaction or appreciation from their services are not going to volunteer again and will eventually result in declining membership for organizations such as Rotary.

The declining figures in the 2000 NSGVP (Statistics Canada, 2001) contrast with the theories of Halman (2003), who suggested that economic development tends to produce rising levels of volunteering (p. 185). Putnam (2000) suggested that many civic associations, such as service clubs (e.g., Rotary, Kiwanis, and Lions), which were once active in mobilizing volunteer services, have experienced falling levels in the United States (p. 117). The 2000 NSGVP also stated a similar decline in volunteer participation in Canada.

Therefore, to retain its members, the Rotary Club must ensure that volunteers and their interests are known and respected. Volunteers want a sense of their own place and a chance to advance to serving on committees, on boards, and in other responsible positions. The volunteer organization must ensure "there is a formal vehicle by which the volunteers have a voice in the policy development as it affects their ranks (Wolf, 1999, p. 106). DePree's (2003) opinion was that organizations need to make it their business to care about the people they have working for them, as well as the people they serve, which is the basis for success and service (p. 91). The volunteer joins the organization as he or she wants meaningful responsibility and to be taken seriously in their involvement. A successful volunteer organization gives its members the opportunity to become involved and achieve their goals.

Statistics Canada (2001) succinctly described volunteers as:

Caring and involved Canadians give, volunteer and participate to support and connect with individuals, groups and communities. They offer their time, skills and compassion. They donate money to organizations and causes to support efforts that they and their families value most. Their contributions add to the quality of life of individuals and to the health of their communities. Their actions help define who we are as Canadians (p. 55).

Volunteers in the Rotary Club do not receive wages. Dekker and Halman (2003) stated, because volunteers do not have the satisfaction of a pay check they have to get more satisfaction out of their contributions of service to help others (p. 2). To counteract the threat of declining volunteers, the organizations must focus its mandate on the reasons for volunteering as it relates to the volunteers' goals, values, and concerns about the quality of life in the community, while offering the individual an opportunity to be involved for personal satisfaction and for giving service to the community.

The Community

Volunteers want to give something back to improve the community. "They are concerned about the quality of life in their community. They want to participate in a meaningful way, give something back, improve the community by identifying new social issues and gaps in service" (MacLeod & Hogarth, 1999, p. 5). Social capital of volunteer organizations gives great benefits to the community. As a result of the time and service of volunteers, social capital within the community is created.

"Leisure volunteering as social capital constitutes an enormous reservoir of skills, energy, and local and special interest knowledge" (Stebbins, 2004, p. 241). In volunteer organizations, leaders teach their volunteers the ability to perform and to achieve, not by control or instruction, but by giving successful examples of themselves. These services provided by the volunteers to the community create social capital of the volunteer organizations and ultimately value to the community.

Social Capital of Volunteer Organizations

Social capital, according to Ladd (1999), encompasses any form of citizens' civic engagement to address community needs and problems and to enhance community life (p. 3). Putman (2000) similarly stated that "altruism, volunteering, and philanthropy—our readiness to help others—is by some interpretations, a central measure of social capital" (p. 116). Social capital enhances productivity of an organization by increasing the volunteers' ability to achieve a given set of objectives. For example, "people who trust each other and cooperate easily and more frequently and, can readily achieve their objectives (Beem, 1999, p. 20). My research will investigate if organizations such as Rotary, build social capital within a community.

The influence of social capital upon volunteer organizations is seen in Putnam's (2000) example of the family as a key form of social capital (p. 73). In volunteer organizations, Devlyn (2001) used the example of Rotary as ordinary people from various cultures and nationalities, who will put aside their differences and prejudices so as to better understand one another. Their ultimate joy of serving is from helping those less fortunate (p. xxvi). In paralleling these thoughts, Butcher (2003) expressed that volunteerism creates the proper environment for interpersonal relations to flourish. These relationships are beneficial for both the volunteer and those who receive the volunteer services (p. 117).

Although relationships are recognized as beneficial and mandatory, it is equally important to be cognizant that, although social capital is positive, as in mutual support, cooperation, trust, and institutional effectiveness, it can also have negative ramifications, as with malevolent, antisocial purposes that lead to outcomes, such as seen in the Ku Klux Klan organizations (Putnam, 2000, p. 22). It is important to be cognizant and recognize the two aspects of social capital and be aware of their dangers.

Therefore, it is imperative that the community needs to build up the benevolent social capital by restoring those institutions that are most able to create social capital. "Civil society advocates maintain that our sorry social conditions results from a depletion of social capital. And if we are to rectify this condition, they argue, we must restore those institutions that are most able to create social capital" (Beem, 1999, p. 162).

Rotary is an example of an organization that creates and possesses social capital that provides beneficial services to the community. Volunteering means participation and cooperation, which creates trust in people who also benefit from voluntary work. "The presence of social capital facilitates participation in voluntary activities and membership of voluntary associations" (Voicu & Voicu, 2003, p. 145). The dedicated volunteer sector "delivers a wide variety of services, some of which are not delivered elsewhere," nor delivered as well (Gann, 1996, p. 105). Rotary's strength is the networks of ordinary people around the world, "who commit their surplus time and energies to a cause, on their own initiative and free will" (Beck, 2005, p. 170). Similarly, Tretter and Tuttle (2005) described the service of volunteer organizations as an opportunity for people to make a difference. They suggested volunteers make the most of this opportunity through extending one's "most valued resources of time and talent" (p. 108). Beem supported the belief that social capital "enhances productivity, for it increases a group's ability to achieve a given set of objectives" (p. 20). In the view of academic writers, people who trust each other cooperate more easily and more frequently, thereby, are able to achieve their objectives (Beck; Beem; Decker & Halman; Gann; Tretter & Tuttle).

The concept of social capital is to maintain trust, cooperation, respect for one another, and a belief that mankind is good and that service to one's community will bring benefits to both the volunteer as well as those who receive the volunteer services. Rotary is fortunate to attract volunteers whose experiences and expertise vastly contributes to its world goals of health, literacy, peace, and friendship, as well as contribute greatly to its respective communities with relevant projects and services that are appropriate for that community.

Social capital within Rotary is what makes it such a valuable organization, and an example was illustrated by the Polio Plus campaign to eradicate Polio throughout the world.

> In the 1980s, 1,000 children were infected by the disease every day in 125 countries. Today, polio cases have declined by 99 percent, with fewer than two thousand cases reported in 2006. Two billion children have been immunized, 5 million have been spared disability, and more than 250,000 deaths from polio have been prevented (Rotary International, 2007a, Polio section, ¶ 15).

The past President of Rotary International has captured the true essence of Rotary by his comments:

> Rotarians have accomplished a feat unmatched in human history. They have immunized 2 billion children against polio by immunizing 100 million children in a single day in places like India and Nigeria. It is the goal of Rotary to eradicate polio by 2005, the 100th Anniversary of Rotary (Devlyn, 2001, p. 106).

Just as Rotary International has accomplished commendable feats, I believe that local Rotary Clubs can also follow their example. To accomplish this, my research endeavoured to identify how the Rotary Club can best expand its volunteer services to its community and challenge the organization to its utmost beneficial services, through use of valuable social capital that exists within Rotary Clubs and the Rotary Club of Prince Rupert.

Social Capital as Value to the Community

Dekker and Halman (2003) identified social capital of the community as services delivered to those in need, through activities that would not have been available without volunteers (p. 8). It is imperative that volunteer organizations give volunteers the opportunity to participate and contribute, by providing the channel for skills, aspirations, interest, and concerns for which they may not have an outlet through their work or home life. As well, volunteers join organizations as they want new experiences, challenges, personal development, career contacts, and new friends.

"The key to attracting volunteers is convincing them that your organization has something to offer them as volunteers and something to offer the community" (MacLeod & Hogarth, 1993, p. 96). Volunteer organizations offer tremendous benefits to the volunteers, while delivering beneficial products and services to the community. For these reasons, service organizations, such as Rotary, give volunteers the opportunity to achieve their goals and needs, while giving valuable service to their communities

My research question was developed to identify how the volunteers and their organization can reach their goals in service to the community. The purpose of this literature review was to research what the academic authors said about volunteer organizations, reasons for their being, their leadership, and the reason why people volunteer to contribute for the benefit of the community. The literature review confirmed that volunteer organizations give people the opportunity to bring together their talents and expertise, and many people working together can make a big difference in what they can accomplish. However, the leadership of volunteer organizations can be very challenging, and leaders need to be cognizant that adults see and understand differently from one another due to generational personalities, educational background, and cultural differences.

This research project endeavoured to find the means for the Rotary Club of Prince Rupert to benefit the organization, the volunteers, and the community. This process of literature review set the framework for my community-based action research, to identify how the Rotary Club of Prince Rupert can best expand its volunteer service to the community. As a result, I have established the research approach, methodology, and the process of data analysis to discover and identify what positive changes can be initiated within the organization.

CHAPTER THREE: RESEARCH APPROACH AND METHODOLOGY

I have chosen community-based action research for my research methodology as it best described my desire to engage all stakeholders in the process of investigation. Stringer (1999) stated, "as an evolving approach to inquiry, community-based action research speaks to the current crisis of research by envisaging a collaborative approach to investigation that seeks to engage 'subjects' as equal and full participants in the research process" (p. 9). "The primary purpose is as a practical tool for solving problems experienced by people in their professional, community or private lives" (p. 11).

This research approach as described by Stinger was the most appropriate to answer my research question: "How can the Rotary Club of Prince Rupert best expand its volunteer services to the community?" The desired outcome of my research project was to discover and identify what positive changes can be initiated within the organization and, thereby, benefit the members, the organization, and the community. Stringer stated, "If an action research project does not make a difference, in a specific way, for practitioners and/or clients, then it has failed to achieve its objectives" (p. 11).

To ensure my study made a difference for the members of the Rotary Club, I prepared the following research design and plan to identify how I needed to proceed and the steps to follow to achieve the intended objectives. The purpose of the research design was to plan the study conduct, document the data, and ensure validity and authenticity of the data, while implementing ethical considerations throughout the entire process.

Overview of the Research Design

Research, to be credible, must be carefully planned, laid out, inspected, and approved by others (Leedy & Ormrod, 2005, p. 115). They further stated research would be much more efficient and effective by identifying the resources, procedures, and data and always with the central goal of the research question foremost in mind (p. 85). It was necessary to ensure the research plan reflected how I was to address my research questions. These research questions endeavoured to discover and identify what organizational changes were required of the Rotary Club that would be necessary to best expand the volunteer services to the community.

"Experienced researchers also know that research most often comes together when they have a plan" (Booth, Colomb, & Williams, 2003, p. 3). However, I needed to be cognizant that, however carefully I planned, the research would not necessarily allow me to stay directly on that path. "Research follows a crooked path, taking unexpected turns, even looping back on itself" (p. 5). As complex as that process was, a basic plan ensured I did not lose my way on this journey. "When you can manage the parts, you can manage the whole" (p. 5).

I reviewed the research design defined by Morgan (1997), who stated the purpose was to plan how the data were to be collected, who would be the participants, how the groups would be structured, the level of moderator involvement and the size and number of each group needed to be determined before beginning the project (p. 34). Leedy and Ormrod (2005) stressed a similar procedure: "The research design provides the overall structure for the procedures the research follows, the data the researcher collects, and the data analysis the researcher conducts" (p. 85).

Therefore, my research design was devised using similar procedures to ensure I obtained the data required to reached the goals of this study and found the answers to my research question as to how the Rotary Club can best expand its volunteer services to the community. As this research project involved both the Rotary Clubs and the community, it was necessary I understood each of the methods to effectively determine the method most appropriate for the wide range of participants. These participants included members of two Rotary Clubs, service providing organizations, the City Council and administration staff, and the citizens.

It was appropriate that I initially studied qualitative, quantitative, and mixed methods to ensure I understood and selected the most appropriate methodology. Once I had identified the research methodology I would use, I was able to identify the research methods and tools to be used, the procedures I would follow, and how I would perform the data analysis. The study conduct explained how the participants were selected; the reasons for selecting focus groups, interviews, World Café, and surveys used for data collection; explanation of the documentation of the data; and the ethical issues considered and implemented. To enable me to proceed, I determined that a literature review of qualitative, quantitative, and mixed methods was the most appropriate way to begin.

Qualitative, Quantitative, and Mixed Research Methods

The decision to use the community-based action research was the result of the evaluation of qualitative, quantitative, and mixed methods. It was very important that I understood these methods to ensure I selected the most appropriate method(s) for my research and one that would produce the data to address my research question. Creswell (2003) stated the choice of which approach to use is based on the research problem, personal experiences, and the audiences for whom one seeks to write (p. 23). Therefore, I conducted further literature reviews as to what the authors stated about each of these methods.

Qualitative inquiry is one method in community-based action research and is defined by Glesne (2006) as ever changing (p. 19). Leedy and Ormrod (2005) defined qualitative research as "used to answer questions about the complex nature of the phenomena, often with the purpose of describing and understanding the phenomena from the participant's point of view" (p. 94). Wolcott (2001) stated, "Qualitative approaches beckon because they appear natural, straightforward, even 'obvious' and thus easy to accomplish" (p. 7). I concurred with Leedy and Ormrod that qualitative research understands the phenomena from the participant's point of view, and I endeavoured to keep this foremost in my process of research

In contrast to qualitative research, "quantitative research is used to answer questions about relationships among measurable variables with the purpose of explaining, predicting and controlling phenomena" (Leedy & Ormrod, 2005, p. 94). They defined the distinguishing characteristics of quantitative research as having structured guidelines for conducting research. As noted by Leedy and Ormrod, concepts, variable hypotheses, and methods of measurement tend to be defined before the study begins and remain the same throughout. The researcher tries to remain detached from the participants, so that they can draw unbiased conclusions (p. 95).

Whereas, Leedy and Ormrod (2005) viewed the qualitative research process as more holistic and emergent with the specific focus, design, measurement instruments, (e.g. interviews) and interpretations developing and possibly changing along the way. "The researcher, though being of open mind, immerses himself or herself in the complexity of the situation and interacts with their participants" (p. 95). According to Creswell (2003), "a mixed method design is useful to capture the best of both quantitative and qualitative approaches" (p. 22). He explained this by stating, "A researcher may want to both generalize the findings to a population and develop a detailed view of the meaning of a phenomenon or concept for individuals" (p. 22).

However, due to the diversity of the target groups, my research required consistency for all research groups and participants, in order to achieve the data I needed to realistically answer my research question. Having read and studied the literature on qualitative, quantitative, and mixed method research, my decision was to conduct my project by qualitative, community-based action research as it was most appropriate for my research. Having made the selection to use the community-based action research, therefore, determined the research methods and tools I would select to conduct my study.

Research Methods and Tools

The research methods and tools I selected were to ensure that I obtained credible, comprehensive, and unbiased input. The general tool of research, according to Leedy and Ormrod (2005), is a "specific mechanism or strategy the researcher uses to collect, manipulate, or interpret data" (p. 12). They listed such tools as the library and its resources, the computer and its software, techniques of measurement, statistics, the human mind, and the language as examples of tools. The major tools that I used were text books, Internet, use of computer and software, measurement, the human mind, and language.

Inquiry tools consisted of pre-established research questions developed with my project sponsor and project supervisor and pre-tested with a wide selection of fellow learners at Royal Roads University, who provided me their written comments. The questions were also pre-tested with non-Rotarians and Rotarians for clarity and ease of understanding. Similar questions were asked for each of the research groups to ensure consistency and validity of data. Krueger (1998) stressed that wording of the questions must be "direct, forthright, comfortable, and simple" (p. 3).

The desired outcome of the research methods and tools was to obtain consistent and valid data. "The more valid and reliable our measurement instruments are, the more likely we are to draw appropriate conclusions form the data we collected and, thus, to solve our research problem in a credible fashion" (Leedy & Ormrod, 2005, p. 93). Therefore, following their advice, I used procedures that ensured the validity of data crucial to my project by the recording of comprehensive, accurate notes and observations during meetings and events. Through established procedures for the data collection, data reliability was achieved through the use of consistent questions and standardization of data collection from each method and person.

Procedures for Data Collection

Before any commencement of the data collection, it was imperative that a letter of consent be signed (see Appendices A, B, C, D, and E) to ensure that the participant clearly understood his or her rights to withdraw at any time and that participation was absolutely voluntary. It was also important to explain that, once the process has commenced, it may not be possible to remove the information given by that participant, as the comments were not identified according to speaker. Participants were also assured that once the research was completed, all data collected would be destroyed and at no time in the research or reports would the participant be identified. Confidentiality was the utmost consideration, and at no time would names be mentioned or identity of the participants recorded.

After I advised the participants, being interviewed and they made their decision to participate by their own free will and choice, I held the focus group, World Café, interviews, and surveys to obtain the raw data. This data were then subjected to comprehensive and detailed analysis to endeavour to find the answer to my research question, "How can the Rotary Club of Prince Rupert best expand its volunteer services to the community?"

Data Analysis

Therefore, to make sense of what I have seen, heard, and read, the data analysis was conducted according to Glesne (2006), who identified the need to "categorize, synthesize, search for patterns, and interpret the data that have been collected" (p. 147). Working with the data, I used the same theme process for data collected from the Board members, who participated in the focus group, and the club members, who participated in the World Café. I realized the importance of describing how I analyzed the data; documented what I did to sort, categorize, and theme the raw data; and how I arrived at the themes or summary data statements based on the analysis. This section is important in establishing the validity of the findings and conclusions.

I created a database of all the notes, observations, and information collected during the study conduct. Once this was done, I created two separate databases. One was the overall database, and the other was divided into the method of collecting that data. For example, I created one database for the focus group, another for the World Café, and one for the interviews. The surveys were kept separately in service provider organizations. Krueger (1998) stated, "The researcher can sort, categorize, and rearrange statements with ease" (p. 57) with the use of the computer. Krueger also discussed how the use of "colored paper and colored markers are helpful for keeping track of different categories" (p. 57). He also went into cutting and pasting the document: "This low technology option has been used in countless analysis projects, and it allows the analyst to identify themes and categorize results" (p. 57). However, I decided that I would use both the computer and written documentation to prepare the database.

Having developed a database, each category was read and re-read to assemble common themes within that category in accordance to the criteria established for each theme. This criterion is itemized in chapter four. Krueger (1998) suggested researchers "analyze question by question, looking for themes, within questions and then across questions" (p. 73), such as what themes emerge from the responses. I proceeded in this manner by writing the comments and responses from each question. I chose not to do this on the computer as I am very visual and tactile, and the hands-on writing helped me to understand more clearly.

Each journal page was given a specific question asked at each event. I documented themes from the first event. The focus group answers were recorded for each question. I then repeated the same process for the World Café, interviews, and the survey—each with its own page for each question.

Next, I took the same questions from each event's page, and I merged the data onto one page related to that question. I compared the emerging themes to each question and determined the common themes within that question.

Once I had all the themes from each question, I then refined the themes more concisely and used only the data that reflected the general comments of each group. Throughout this process of data analysis, I held the ethical issues and requirements foremost during the analysis and documentation. As required, I established principles, practices, and procedures that ensured ethical conduct of the research, including confidentiality of the data. Krueger (1998) gave the example:

> Participants tell about their behaviours or experiences, and if shared publicly, these could prove to be harmful. Confidentiality was promised. This means that no names are attached to reports and the speaker cannot be identified by other situational or contextual factors (p. 76).

Nancy Eidsvik, MA

Once the data were collected from the focus group meeting, the interviews, World Café, and surveys, "the task of the researcher facilitator in this phase of the research process is to interpret and render understandable the problematic experiences being considered" (Stringer, 1999, p. 90). Stringer further explained, "Interpretation builds on description through conceptual frameworks—definitions and framework of meaning—that enable participants to make better sense of their experiences" (p. 90). In order for me to do this, I needed to understand definitions and frameworks of meaning, so that as a researcher, I provided the opportunity for participants to understand their own experiences as to what made sense to them.

Within community-based action research, "stakeholders participate in a process of rigorous inquiry, acquiring information (collecting data) and reflecting on that information (analyzing) to transform their understanding about the nature of the problem, under investigation (theorizing)" (Stringer, 1999, p. 10). The study conduct presents how I collected the raw data and analyzed the data from the focus groups, one-on-one interviews, World Café, and surveys to understand the nature of the problem I was researching.

Study Conduct

The information from the first focus group and the World Café resulted from the participation of the Rotary Club members. The club is comprised of 58 members. The leadership of the organization is through the President and 10 directors who make up the Board of Directors. The Board is responsible to all the members of the Club. From within the membership, the Board of Directors appoints Chairs of various committees and committee members. Through their Chair, committees report to the Board of Directors and subsequently to the members, though this is not necessarily done on a regular or on-going basis.

This study conduct encompassed the review of the organizational structure through the chosen methodology of community-based action research. The collection of data was through focus group, World Café, interviews, and surveys. Also discussed was how the participants were selected and invited, the ethical issues, and the data collection and analysis. It was imperative that, as the researcher, I be cognizant that the credibility of my report can be weakened if the data are perceived to be biased (Leedy & Ormord, 2005, p. 209). They further stated that, "what is unprofessional, however, is for the researcher to fail to acknowledge the likelihood of biased data or to fail to recognize the possibility of bias in the study" (p. 210).

It is hoped that, as the researcher, I would be seen as one who is knowledgeable about Rotary and shares the concern that volunteer organizations must grow, serve, and be successful to survive. It was the intent of my research study to identify how volunteer organizations can strive to be successful. I am aware that any perceived impartiality in obtaining relevant data for my research may be an important factor.

Therefore, the conduct of the study was to ensure credible, trustworthy, and unbiased data to produce a research report that will have value to the members of Rotary. To ensure value to Rotary members, my research design studied how the project participants were selected and established the criteria for that selection process.

Project Participants

My decision to use the qualitative, community-based action research determined the participants I invited to participate in my research. Stringer (1999) stated that researchers "need to identify and communicate with people in positions of influence and authority (p. 52). In addition, it was important that I obtain information as to how the Rotary Club was viewed by those in the community. This information was sought from the members of the City Council, senior management staff of the City of Prince Rupert (City Hall), community service provider organizations, and the citizens at large. During the process, it became evident that input from the other Rotary Club (Hecate Strait Rotary Club) was important. As a result, I obtained permission from my project supervisor to host the second focus group for this club. The information received proved to be what my study required to add to and substantiate various findings.

Including the Hecate Strait Rotary members, the total of invited participants was 156 persons, with each service provider organization counted as one participant. The invited participants were comprised of: (a) the Executive of the Rotary Club of 11 members; the general membership of the club was 58 members; (b) Hecate Strait Club with 28 members; (c) the City Hall comprised of the Mayor, 6 councillors, and 3 senior city staff; (d) 15 service provider organizations were and;

(e) 10 citizens randomly selected from the general public. The citizens selected were not part of any of the organized groups.

The first focus group was comprised of the Board of Directors of the Prince Rupert Rotary Club, in which eight participated, and I held a follow-up interview with one member. I also held a focus group with members of the Hecate Strait Rotary Club, which was attended by 18 members and guests. The World Café was held for the general membership of the Prince Rupert Rotary Club, in which 44 members and 2 guest Rotarians attended. The one-on-one interviews were conducted on separate occasions with the Mayor and three Councillors and three senior management staff of the City of Prince Rupert. Surveys were distributed to the 15 service provider organizations, of which 10 organizations responded. Of the 132 invited participants, 90 participated with no returned surveys from the citizens.

The invitation to the general public was sent initially to 10 people randomly selected from the telephone directory. There were no responses received. Following discussions with my project supervisor and project sponsor, it was decided that I send another 10 surveys selected from the business community, as it was anticipated that they would be the ones to be involved in community matters. However, no responses were received.

After further discussions with my project supervisor, a further 20 surveys were sent to citizens who I knew to be community minded, but people I did not personally know, to ensure there would be no perceived bias in the data. There were still no responses from the public. I sought advice on the lack of public response from both my project supervisor and my project sponsor.

Initially being concerned about the public interest and awareness of Rotary, I had considered purposive sampling, where people in locations are intentionally sought because they meet some criteria for inclusion in the study (Palys, 2003, p. 142). Palys further stated that target sampling can reflect the understanding of the phenomenon of interests, needs, or wants, and "these purposive choices may indirectly reaffirm rather than challenge the understanding" (p. 142). I had anticipated using purposive sampling but was cautioned by my project supervisor that by using the purposive selection method, the data collected could be perceived as being biased.

There were two other situations in my research where I sought advice from the Ethics Department of Royal Roads University. The first was to obtain permission to use a family member as my research associate. I had selected my daughter, whose experience as a professional consultant in the field of community service would be invaluable to my research. I received permission from the Ethics Committee of Royal Roads University to use the proposed facilitator.

The second advice I sought was regarding consent from the participants for the World Café, as I thought that members would be reluctant to sign a consent form, and I did not wish to jeopardize Rotary members' participation in my data collection. I received permission from the Ethics Committee of Royal Roads University to use one consent form for all the members to sign, and each member also received a copy of the consent form (see Appendix B).

In the interim and during the preparation period, I presented various reports to the membership, explaining the purpose of my project, the involvement of the Rotarians, and the requirement of my obtaining consent forms. I further explained their choice not to participate would not incur any ramifications and the consent form was the requirement of the university. Further to this, each member was advised that he or she could withdraw at any time.

It was very important to my research that I endeavoured and ensured all participants were comfortable with the process and did not feel threatened in any manner (MacKeracher, 2006, p. 126). Therefore, I used great care in planning the focus group, World Café, interviews, and survey. I wanted participants to want to be part of my research and to enjoy the process. It was also very important that I be cognizant that people are not "created equal: some are informative or provocative; others are unwilling to talk" (Palys, 2003, p. 143), and conversely, there are those who talk prolifically and say very little. Since the purpose of my research was to determine how the Rotary Club can best expand its volunteer services to the community, it was important that I receive open and honest input from the members through the focus group held for the Board of Directors.

First Focus Group

The first focus group session was attended by eight members of the board. Krueger (1994) stated, "Focus groups are best conducted with participants who are similar to each other. . . . [The] strength for focus groups are their reliance on interaction in the group to produce the data" (p. 14). There is the corresponding weakness is that the "group itself may influence the nature of the data it produces" (Morgan, 1997, p. 15). There is also concern that participants may hesitate to make negative or controversial comments as their opinions are heard by all those in attendance. This raises privacy concerns and can limit the kind of topics that can be pursued (p. 31). However, participants of both focus groups had no hesitation in acknowledging issues of concern and were very candid in their comments.

To ensure attendance, I personally invited each board member to attend the focus group. Also, three weeks prior to each focus group, the board members were officially invited by letter to participate in the session (see Appendix F). The agenda and questions were well established in advance (see Appendix G), and the meeting was efficiently organized.

Because the facilitator was experienced and knowledgeable, she conducted the focus group with ease and professionalism. Her style of conducting the meeting was sincere and warm, which quickly placed the participants at ease. She welcomed them to the focus group and explained the process and order of the meeting.

To create and maintain an informal atmosphere, her style of presenting the pre-established questions was conversational as befitted a social gathering (Krueger, 1998, p. 3). The opening question was not intended to obtain information but rather to set the atmosphere. Once the participants became comfortable and enthusiastic as to the process, the facilitator moved onto the next question called the introductory question. This gave the participants the opportunity to reflect on their experiences as well as to get to know what others felt or believed. The next step is called the "transition question," which begins to focus on the key questions of the study. This portion of the discussion was given the most time so all participants were able to participate and contribute. Once the established time to end the meeting was near, the facilitator moved the discussions to the ending question to bring the meeting to closure. Following, this, the facilitator adeptly summarized the discussions offering the participants the opportunity to agree, correct, or add further thoughts and comments (pp. 23–26).

The value of a professional facilitator was the ease with which the meeting proceeded and the enthusiasm and eagerness of the participants. The facilitator ensured timing and clarity of purpose was maintained to keep the meeting flowing smoothly and effectively. Throughout the meeting, the facilitator asked individual participants for his or her comments. Everyone was given equal opportunity to contribute, and yet no one was coerced to speak or comment.

Numerous times the facilitator asked if there was anything different participants would like to see or do, but the meeting continued with everyone seeming to like most things about Rotary. It was not until almost the end of the session, when one comment about lack of participation by some members brought about a flood of comments about how "only 10 percent of the members seem to do all the work." As a result of this line of discussions, I added a question to the World Café to ask the members if "there was one thing they could change about Rotary, what that would be?" (see Appendix G)

As the researcher, it was difficult to sit back and not be involved, but it was important that I not be perceived as having influence, and I wanted all participants to feel free to comment as they wished. I was cognizant to be careful, as Stringer (1999) cautioned, not to impose my opinions on others or use it as a tool to define the reality of the situation (p. 59). Therefore, my role at the focus group was to remain at the back of the room and take notes on comments and observations. In contrast, it was interesting to note that Morgan (1997) believed that "there is no hard evidence that the moderator's impact on the data is any greater than the researcher's impact on participant's observation" (p. 14).

To ensure that documentation of the discussions were accurate, I used an electronic recorder, very small and highly sensitive, to record the discussions. "The use of a tape recorder has the advantage of allowing the researcher to record accounts that are both detailed and accurate" (Stringer, 1999, p. 70). However, it is very important that the recorder not be imposing and distract from the participation. "People sometimes find it difficult to talk freely, in the presence of a recording device" (p. 71). I asked participants for permission to use the recorded in advance of the meeting, to which they all agreed that it would not cause a problem in their discussions. It was also very important that the recorder had ample tape to record so that the meeting would not be disturbed by having to change the tape. To also ensure that there would be no equipment failure, I had a second recorder to use as backup if required. To ensure that the meeting was ready when participants arrived and equipment was working, I arrived one hour before the session, to set up the room and test all the equipment and supplies.

To add to the ambience and to set a social atmosphere, snacks, fruit, dessert, soft drinks, and water were provided, as food encourages relaxation and discussions. Krueger and Casey (2000) stated that "food can help the focus group. Eating together tends to promote conversation and communication within the group" (p. 104). The result was a relaxed and informal meeting, with a social atmosphere that produced an enormous amount of information. Morgan (1997) stated, "It is the researcher's interest that provides the focus, whereas the data themselves come from group interaction" (p. 6).

The meeting was scheduled for one and a half hours and began precisely on time and concluded on time. Being punctual was very important to the success of this meeting. Also, participants had been advised when invited as to the length of the meeting. It was also important that participants received the draft notes of the meeting, which was shared with them within two days following the event. Each board member was invited to submit additional information or corrections to my notes. There were no responses to this request. However, many expressed their interest in participating in the World Café and were genuinely looking forward to it.

World Café

Following the focus group meeting, the World Café was held for the general membership. Several months prior to the scheduled World Café, I was given the opportunity to speak at a noon Rotary meeting. At that time, I explained what a World Café was and how I planned to obtain information from the members. The date for the World Café was set and announced to the members. Frequently during this period, I spoke personally to many members who were interested in the World Café. I also reminded the members at each noon meeting of the scheduled World Café and the reasons for the required consent forms.

One week prior to the World Café, I emailed an invitation (see Appendix H) to all members of the Rotary Club with an attached consent form (see Appendix B), to give them time to read and understand the form. I also invited anyone with questions to contact me at the phone number or email I had listed. Initially, I had intended to obtain one consent form signed by all members in attendance; this was approved by the Royal Roads University Ethics Committee. I was concerned that members would oppose having to sign a form just to participate in my World Café. However, at the World Café, many members handed in their signed consent forms, leading me to decide to obtain one consent form from each member, as I did not sense any reluctance in their providing me with this document. My research assistant and I were prepared with ample consent forms for everyone not having one. Each person willingly signed the form, and it was the responsibility of my assistant to ensure that all consent forms were signed and submitted to her.

Determining the right participants for the World Café was very important. Since every member of the Rotary Club was invited to participate, they were the right participants. "Diversity of thought and experience is perhaps the single most important criterion for gaining new insight and accessing collective wisdom" (Brown & Isaacs, 2005, p. 53).

Accessing of this wisdom and insight is obtained through its participants "moving among tables, talking with new people, contributing your thinking, and linking the essence of your discoveries to ever widening circles of thought are hallmarks of the World Café" (Brown & Isaacs, 2005, p. 169). I chose World Café for the members of the Rotary Club, as "an individual World Café conversation can create a rich web of unexpected insights though the cross-pollination of ideas and the creations of new personal networks" (p. 190).

Most Rotarians are very busy people whose lives are dominated by work and family, as well as other organizations on which they serve. For these reasons, I chose to hold the World Café during a regular noon meeting, which would be convenient and interesting for the members. I arranged with the Club President that the meeting was to commence promptly at 12:00 noon and conclude at 1:15 PM, with no Rotary business being scheduled. I would have preferred two hours for the World Café, but I knew that members would not be able to meet for that long.

Three weeks prior to the World Café, I discussed the menu with the chef of the facility, who was familiar with hosting such an event. We decided to serve six varieties of pizza, "pretend beer" (soft drinks and juice), and dessert. This proved to be highly successful and many positive comments were received.

As the name World Café signifies food and social fun, it was important that it be planned to run smoothly and without interruption. Therefore, the day of the World Café, my assistant and I ensured the room was set up so that eight people could be seated at each table, and participants were seated at random in order of their arrival to the meeting. The agenda was posted outside the meeting room, as well as a copy for each participant (see Appendix I). The entrance to the room was decorated as a café would be. On each table, we had placed snack food of fruit and nuts just as one would expect of a café.

Once the atmosphere was set and the members arrived, it was evident that they were caught up in the setting and mood of the event. Questions for the World Café (see Appendix J) were at each table, and the agenda was posted throughout the room. A board member (director) was assigned to facilitate and another director to record at each table. I selected the directors, as they had already participated in the focus group. It was appropriate that they be assigned duties, and they were obviously pleased with these duties and responsibilities. Each table had pre-assigned questions (chosen from Appendix J), arranged for interest on brightly coloured poster boards and with ample room to write. Participants were also encouraged to write, and coloured pens were available at each table. Participants were given 10 minutes at each table and were then asked to change tables. This process was repeated four times. To conclude, a summary period was held for each table to report to the general meeting. "The World Café is designed to foster collective knowledge-sharing and knowledge creation; no individual is as likely to make these discoveries alone" (Brown & Isaacs, 2005, p. 149).

> Brown and Isaacs (2005) expressed my desire to give people the opportunity to experience the mutual contribution, connectedness, community and commitment that the World Café fosters, it is my deepest hope that many more of us—whatever our national identities or political persuasions—will value and embrace the culture of connection as one path to a life-affirming future for us all (p. 105).

As with the other events held, a written draft report was given to all the members the following day, with a request for additions, corrections, or clarifications. There were no responses to this request other than to express appreciation for the enjoyment of the event and the new learning some of them gained. I received the following email comment following the World Café.

> This World Café was an opportunity for us to ground ourselves and get back to the basics. A chance for each of us to re-evaluate the reasons we joined Rotary and to re-commit to ourselves and the club that we want to be active participants and be part of the "giving back" that Rotary does both locally and internationally. I hope we've been helpful to you, because I really got the feeling that through this exercise, you've helped each of us and the club in general (World Café participant).

This concluded the information gathering from the members of the Rotary Club. Interviews were then conducted to obtain information from those outside of Rotary and addressed their perspectives of the club's services and its value to the community.

Interviews

Simultaneously with the World Café and first focus group, the one-on-one interviews were held with members of the City Council and senior administration staff of City Hall, which invited input as to their perception of the services performed by the Rotary Club to the community. "Interviews enable participants to describe their situation" (Stringer, 1999, p. 68). The process not only "provides a record of their view and perspective, but also symbolically recognizes the legitimacy of their view" (p. 68). The intent of the interviews was to collect opinions and information from people who represent the citizens and are most aware of the situation within the community. Morgan (1997) confirmed the value of interviews and stated, "Other distinct advantages of individual interviews occur when the goal of the research is to gain in depth understanding of a person's opinion and experiences" (p. 11).

In preparation for the interviews, I contacted each member of the City Council by email two weeks in advance and requested an appointment, explaining my research project and the input that I wished from each of them (see Appendix K). I advised them I did not wish to distribute the questions in advance, as I desired spontaneity of responses. To ensure consistency of data, I had pre-established questions (see Appendix L), consistent with the questions I had asked the Rotarians. Each interviewee signed a Letter of Consent (see Appendix C) prior to commencing the interviews. To respect their time, I met individually with the Councillors and Mayor for 30 minutes. This was more than sufficient to obtain their thoughts and comments, as they are knowledgeable of their expectations and desires for both the community and how Rotary can best serve the people. Those participants who wished longer to discuss related matters were given additional time for conversation.

As each interview was completed, a draft summary of my notes was sent to each participant for review and comments, and at that time I thanked each one for his or her time and sharing information and experiences. Each interviewee responded that the information was correct as recorded. During these interviews, the first focus group, and the World Café, it was interesting to hear comments from many of the participants that they believed there could be some way for the two Rotary Clubs in Prince Rupert to work together in more activities and services.

Second Focus Group

As a result of the first focus group, the World Café, and interviews, it became apparent that it was important to obtain information from the Rotary Club of Prince Rupert, Hecate Strait (Hecate Strait Rotary Club). The Hecate Strait Rotary Club is the alternate Rotary Club in Prince Rupert and has 28 members. Themes that arose from the first focus group and World Café sessions indicated that there was a need for the two Rotary Clubs to work together, to ensure there was no duplication of services and to identify the many joint activities that could benefit the community.

I obtained approval from my project supervisor to hold a focus group meeting with the Hecate Strait Rotary Club. I used similar questions as with the other meetings, but also added an extra one addressing the issue of how the two clubs can work together (see Appendix M).

I arranged with the Hecate Strait Rotary Club to hold a focus group meeting at their regular noon meeting. I selected a noon meeting, as it was important that I have participation and input from as many of their members as possible. To ensure that I communicated my desire for the meeting, I spoke at their general noon meeting prior to focus group and explained its purpose to assist me with my research project. The following week, the invitations were sent (see Appendix F) inviting each member to the event with a consent form attached (see Appendix

D). I explained about the consent forms and that their choice whether to participate or not would have no repercussions.

The focus group was started at precisely noon and the questions were posted on the wall (see Appendix M). As facilitator, I asked each question individually, which were then discussed by the group. One of the participants of the second focus group acted as the scribe who recorded all the comments of the participants. The group exuded enthusiasm and gave very sincere and candid comments. At the conclusion of the meeting, many of the members expressed appreciation for the opportunity to participate and several comments were made that it was very informative. The following day, all members of the Hecate Strait Rotary were sent copies of the notes taken by one of their members. Most of the respondents expressed appreciation for the opportunity to be involved. This focus group concluded the face-to-face portion of the data collection.

Surveys

As well as Rotarians, it was important that others from the community were involved. Surveys were developed during my second residency of this Master of Arts in Leadership and Training Program at Royal Roads University (residency two) and pilot tested with members of the cohort. They provided the feedback and suggestions to finalize the questions. Surveys stated response to the questionnaires constituted consent to use their information. Surveys were sent to 15 service provider organizations and nine responses were received. Each organization could represent a wide range of members, but were counted as only one response. These organizations within Prince Rupert are very committed to the needs of the community and people and very knowledgeable of the needs and social conditions. I used a survey as I desired to obtain input from the greatest number of people. These groups have direct contact with the social challenges of the people as well as the humanistic understanding of their needs. As Rotary does not contribute to individual persons, it is these organizations who can benefit most from the funds and services from Rotary and pass these funds onto those who need it the most.

The survey invitations (see Appendix N) sent to service provider organizations elicited feedback from several of the service organizations that I had not attached the survey questions. I realized that they were waiting for the questions and were not responding to the invitation to participate. I obtained permission from my project supervisor to forward survey questions with the acknowledgment letter (see Appendix O) to the service provider organizations. This revised package included the consent to use the information (see Appendix E). Because the Rotary Club does not contribute funds or give assistance to individual people, I anticipated that 10 citizens, randomly selected for their community knowledge, could provide me with the information I required, primarily of their knowledge of the community and the ability to give me meaningful information. I mailed the survey to them, with a return envelope and asked for a response within 15 days.

As I did not receive any responses from the 10 surveys I had sent, I subsequently sent another 30 surveys but still received no responses. The researcher needs to consider causes or reasons why the respondents did not reply. Because I was very cognizant of the Royal Roads University (2007) ethics policy that participants are not required to participate and do so without undue influence and are free to refuse, I did not wish to do the follow up or seem to be pressuring anyone to reply.

Documentation of the Data

Documentation of responses was critical to my research, and survey responses provided me with written documentation of raw data. Krueger (1998) stated that, to capture information, "the choices are memory, field notes, audiotape, videotape and real-time transcription" (p. 73). He recommended that the researcher use as many methods as possible and that multiple methods are preferred.

To document data for the focus groups, I used field notes and audiotape. The notes included observations, verbal information, and general thoughts and comments. The recording device was most valuable. The device was of superior quality and very small in size, so as not to dominate the proceedings, and was very unobtrusive. The value of recording devices was confirmed by Morgan (1997), who stated that "the principal means of capturing observations in a focus group is through audio taping" as credibility and accuracy of the data is of paramount importance (p. 55).

However, for the one-on-one interview, I took notes, as I believed that having a tape recorder would stifle the flow and content of the discussion. To ensure accuracy, at the conclusion of the interview, I summarized what I heard and confirmed with the participant if I had captured the information correctly. Subsequent to the interview, I provided the participant with a copy of my notes to further verify the accuracy.

The World Café notes were recorded by one member at each of the eight tables. At the conclusion of the World Café, a verbal report was also made by each table, so that all participants could be aware of the topics discussed. I subsequently summarized all the notes and distributed them to all the members of the Rotary Club and requested any comments, input, or additional information they wished to make.

The surveys were also very valuable, as the participants not only answered the questions asked, but many times offered additional thoughts and comments. The quality of the responses received from the service provider organizations offered comprehensive and valuable information. The comments from their personal view questions sufficed for the information that I was seeking from the individual citizens.

I assured individuals and organizations who responded to the surveys that the responses would not be seen by anyone other than me as the researcher, thereby emphasizing the confidentiality of the responses

(Leedy & Ormrod, 2005, p. 131). Throughout the study conduct, ethical issues were a priority from the consent forms, confidentiality, the freedom to withdraw, and all the requirements of the various ethics committees and boards.

Ethical Issues

Documentation of the data initiates the importance of ethical issues. The purpose of the *Research Ethics Policy* of the Royal Roads University (2007) "is to establish principles, practices and procedures to guide and ensure the ethical conduct of research and scholarship carried out under the auspices of Royal Roads University" (¶ 1). The general principles stated are "all research and scholarship shall be carried out in accordance with the Tri-Council Policy Statement on Ethical Conduct for Research Involving Humans" (¶ 2), including respect for human dignity, respect for free and informed consent, respect of vulnerable persons, respect for justice and inclusiveness, privacy and confidentiality, balancing harm and benefits, minimizing harm, and maximizing benefits (Canadian Institutes of Health Research, Natural Sciences and Engineering Research Council of Canada, Social Sciences and Humanities Research Council of Canada [Tri-Council], 1998, pp. i.5–i.6).

The American Psychological Association (2001) requires the discussion of confidentiality occur at the outset of the research and thereafter as circumstances may arise (p. 387). The right to privacy is that participants have the right to expect protection of their confidences and preservation of their anonymity (Glesne, 2006, p. 138). Confidentiality means that, as a researcher, I will not discuss with anyone the specifics of what I see and hear. This was imperative in my discussions with the members of the Rotary Club, as well as members of the community. The inquiry into the needs of the community had the potential to uncover confidential and private information in some sectors of the community, especially those who are in need of assistance of either services or funds. As Palys (2003) stated, the researcher has the ethical responsibility to ensure the rights and interests of the participants are protected (p. 102).

Ethics are the most important aspects of my research, as the role of the non-profit society is "profoundly shaped by how they are perceived by the public" (Riggio & Orr, 2004, p. 26). Therefore, it is imperative that as a researcher of a volunteer service organization, I am not only ethical, honest, and trustworthy, but also perceived as being so. To ensure I am compliant with the Code of Ethics, I followed the Royal Roads University (2007) Research Ethics Policy (¶ 14–16), and the guiding ethical principles of the Tri-Council (1998) Policy Statement (pp. i.5–i.6).

In addition to the ethics policy requirements of the Royal Roads University (2007) and the Tri-Council (1998) Policy Statement, I conscientiously implemented the ethics policies of the Declaration of Rotarians in Businesses and Professions (Rotary International, 2007b, p. 79), which requires members to abide by their own professional code of ethics as well as those of Rotary International (2007a) and the Rotary Club of Prince Rupert (2006).

These ethics policies are encompassed in the "Objects of Rotary" (Rotary International, 2007a, ¶ 1–5). The second ethics policy is defined in "The Four-Way Test" (¶ 11). Further to the Rotary ethics standards (Rotary International, 2007a), it was imperative that the information collected for my research was obtained ethically and responsibly and was dependent upon its credibility being unaffected by research bias.

Glesne (2006) wrote that friendship biases can affect data selection and might decrease objectivity (pp. 116–17).

Since Rotary is about friendship, my many years of association with the Rotary Club can certainly be seen as a bias. I have also been involved for many years with a variety of community organizations, and I can be perceived as having established opinions about the community. Leedy and Ormrod (2005) stated that bias attacks the integrity of the facts. Therefore, a researcher must consider the influence of bias on his or her findings and may need to admit the potential bias. By doing this, it gives the readers the option to approve the "research realistically and judge its merits honestly" (p. 210).

Not only is my personal bias open to questions, but also the reader's bias, which may be influence by the recent years of public opinion of the ethical standards of the non profit sector. These standards have become tarnished, which may be due to the actions of a few who have harmed the reputation of the non profit organizations (Riggio & Orr, 2004, p. 26). Unfortunately, I acknowledge the possibility of the Rotary Club can be affected by the same opinion, as there have been a few service organizations within Prince Rupert which have been so involved. Yukl (2006) explained that "the great potential for the misuse of power is one reason so many people are interested in the ethical aspects of leadership" (p. 418). Another reason for this declining public trust has been due to the publicity of scandals in news media and movies (Kouzes & Posner, 2002). Therefore, the success of this study was dependent upon my being seen as an honest, respectful, objective, and a trustworthy researcher.

Success is very important to my research, as the purpose of this study is to improve the services that the Rotary Club provides to the community so that the community will be better served. Stringer (1999) stated that "processes of community-action based research are enriched by researchers who contribute to the lives of the groups with whom they work" (p. 61). As descriptively stated by Booth et al. (2003), "That sense of contributing to a community is never more rewarding than when you can discover something that you believe can improve your readers' lives by changing what and how they think" (p. 8).

My research design and plan laid out the procedures I would use for the data analysis, the study conduct, and the documentation of the data, while ensuring ethical considerations throughout my research project. I have endeavoured to have my research project evolve as a positive experience, while identifying substantive recommendations for organizational improvement to better meet the needs of the community. The research findings and reports are discussed in the following chapters.

CHAPTER FOUR: ACTION RESEARCH PROJECT RESULTS AND CONCLUSIONS

The purpose of this community-based action research study was to find the answer to my research question, "How can the Rotary Club of Prince Rupert best expand its volunteer services to the community?" This study involved two focus groups, a World Café, one-on-one interviews (interviews), and surveys to collect the required data necessary to find answers to my research question. "The goal of combining research methods was to strengthen the total research project, regardless of which method was the primary means of data collection" (Morgan, 1997, p. 23). The data analysis of relying on multiple methods is called triangulation. The methods I used appropriately produced the information, from the perspective of both Rotary Club's members and the community leaders, to answer my research question.

This research has identified the organizational changes required of the Rotary Club to strengthen its organization to thrive and prosper.

This change will produce a committed membership with the ability to provide the services and funds needed to give back to the community.

Study Findings

The study findings report the changes required by the Rotary Club, as identified by the members, other Rotarians, and the community. The changes require the Rotary Club to implement open communication, increase participation, and good leadership to make the organization efficient and effective. An active, vibrant organization will address the issues of increased membership and committed and happy members willing and ready to provide services to fulfill their need to give back to the community. The Rotary Club needs to prepare a concise public-relations plan to inform the public of Rotary's value to the community, the third world countries, and Rotary members. It is important for the Rotary Club to increase the public's awareness of Rotary and to overcome the impression of an exclusive organization. This will, in turn, address the concerns of the decline in Rotary membership, as the citizens of Prince Rupert will be enticed to join.

As stated by Stringer (1999), this research report enables "the researcher to present what they have discovered in their investigation" (p. 178). Stringer further defined community-based action research as presenting narrative accounts that reveal the ways people experience the issue investigated. It describes events, activities and contexts from perspective of the participant (p. 128). To obtain the data to achieve credible results and conclusion, it was imperative to have the participation of service provider organizations, the community, and both Rotary Clubs. Stringer (1999) emphasized,

> Researchers need to ensure that all stakeholders—people whose lives are affected—participate in defining and exploring the problem or service under investigation. Although it is not possible for all people to be thus engaged, it is imperative that all stakeholder groups feel that someone is speaking for their interest and is in a position to inform them of what is going on (p. 49).

Members of the Rotary Club of Prince Rupert (Rotary Club), Rotary Club of Prince Rupert, Hecate Strait (Hecate Strait Rotary Club), City of Prince Rupert (City Hall), and service provider organizations participated in this community-based action research project. The participation demographics are shown in Table 1 (page 127).

As stated, there was excellent participation from all key stakeholders, other than the general public. Rogelberg and Stanton (2007) stated,

> Passive non response does not appear to be planned. Instead, passive non respondents may not have actually received the survey, might have forgotten about it, mislaid it, was ill, or just did not get around to it given other commitments (p. 200).

They go on to state that "bias is not created by passive non respondents" (p. 200). "This does not automatically signify that the data obtained from the research were biased" (p. 198). However, Leady and Ormrod (2005) suggests that survey non response could indicate potential bias could have infiltrated the research design (p. 210).

The impact of bias due to non response from the public was minimized by the participation from City Councillors, senior administration staff at City Hall, and the service provider organizations, all of whom represented the public in this research. Their information adequately provided the views of the general public. "Meetings should reflect the participatory intent of community-based action research, it is important, therefore, to ensure that people who can legitimately speak for the interest of each stakeholding group attend" (Stringer, 1999, p. 82).

Table 1. *Research Participant Demographics*

Participating Groups	Number of Members Invited	Number of Participants	Participation Rate (%)
Focus group: Rotary Club	11	8, plus one follow-up interview	81.8
World Café: Rotary Club	56	44	78.6
Focus group: Hecate Strait Rotary Club	27	17	62.9
Interviews: City Hall councillors and senior staff	9	7	77
Surveys: Service provider organizations	15	11	73.3
Surveys: Members of the community	40	0	0.0
Total	158	88	56

The study findings represent the key issues of participants' shared experiences. I have identified each key issue with its respective theme. For the purpose of this study, I have defined theme as a recurring topic found in the data. These themes emerged in a consistent reoccurring manner regardless of the methods used. Each research question developed the key issues as stated by the participants and from which the themes were identified.

The results are reported in three themes: (a) focus group and World Café meetings; (b) the second focus group; and (c) interviews and surveys, to illustrate the consistency with which these themes arose. It was important and relevant to view the data and information from the perspectives of both Rotarians and the community. These summaries of findings have been consolidated to highlight the common areas of discussions amongst all participants and the themes that resulted from these discussions.

Table 2. *Criteria for Themes*

Theme	Criteria
Communication	Public information
	Public relations
	Public knowledge of Rotary
	Image
	Rotary awareness
	Meeting with another organization

Theme	Criteria
Fellowship, Friendship	Social aspects
	Group activities
	Projects
	Doing things together
	Friendly environment
	Belonging
International service	Projects internationally
Leadership	Committee effectiveness
	Makes difference in people
	Projects funds and application process
	Cooperation
	Share information
	Organize and coordinate service
	Community leaders
	Bring groups together
	Community needs
Learning	Self improvement
	Training
Membership	Member activities
	New members
	Decline in membership
	Member well-being
Partnership	Jointly working with another group

Theme	Criteria
Service	Give back to community
	Members interests
	Member activities
	Projects
	Community benefits
	Major service project
	Make a difference in people's lives

I initially categorized the data into key issues, which I used to define themes and used codes to ensure consistency. For example, the theme "communication" was assigned to those comments that required interaction to accomplish its goal. Participation was initially used when two or more groups were together for a specific purpose. However, as I proceeded with the coding of themes, it became apparent that participation from members should be in all activities, and I chose to not use participation as a theme. Many themes were applicable to one comment, depending upon the assumed intent of the comment. However, it was imperative to remain consistent when assigning each theme.

Table 3. *Consolidated Themes from Focus Groups, World Café, Interviews, and Surveys*

Topic	Key Issues	Themes
What Members like about Rotary	Give back to the community Social aspects International services and projects Learn in a friendly environment Involve everyone	Service Fellowship, Friendship International service, Learning
Improving Member Participation	Rotation of members to committees Good leadership Good communication Image of elitism, businessmen's club, and exclusivity	Fellowship, Friendship Leadership Communication Communication
Changes Members Wanted in the Club	Decline in membership New member orientation Committees function effectively Burn-out of members	Membership Membership Leadership Fellowship, Friendship Leadership Membership
Value of Rotary	Makes a difference in people's lives	Leadership Communication

Topic	Key Issues	Themes
Selection of Funding Recipients	Process and criteria based on merit	Leadership
	Community does not know the process	Leadership
	Standardized, simplified applications	Leadership
	Unbiased selection process	Leadership
Public's Knowledge of the Rotary Club	Generally unaware	Communication
	Those who know about Rotary are impressed	Communication
	Believes the club is exclusive and full of elitists. Exclusive businessmen's club	Communication
Assistance to City Hall	Joint projects with the city	Partnership
	Bring service groups together to strategize activities and projects	Leadership
	Participate in city's five-year plan to help with the youth crime issues	Partnership
		Partnership
		Leadership
How Both Rotary Clubs Can Work Effectively Together	Share information	Partnership
	Establish common goals	Partnership
	Supportive goals and longterm plans	Partnership
	Regular meetings by directors, committee chairs, and the entire membership of each club	Partnership

Topic	Key Issues	Themes
Research Question:	Increase Rotary awareness in community	Communication
"How can the Rotary Club best expand its volunteer service to the community?"	Organizer and coordinate service organizations to avoid duplication	Leadership Partnership
	Shed businessmen's club image	Communication

Table 4. *Focus Groups, World Café, Interviews, and Surveys Frequency of Consolidated Themes*

Theme	Number of Respondents ($N = 75$)
Leadership	11
Communication	8
Partnership	8
Fellowship and friendship	3
Membership	3
Service	2
International service	1
Learning	1

Table 4 describes the consolidation of themes from all the meetings. The criteria of frequency of the themes indicate the importance of leadership, communication, and partnership. The frequency of communication, leadership, and partnership themes by no means indicates a lesser value for fellowship and friendships, service, and learning. These themes are discussed within the research activities that contributed to this report.

Members' Perspectives Using Focus Group and World Café

The Rotary Club focus group and World Café discussions identified the key issues and themes in their responses to the research questions asked at the focus group (see Appendix G) and the World Café (see Appendix J). There were eight focus group participants and a follow-up interview with one of the 11 directors of the Rotary Club. Eight participants of the focus group also attended the World Café. The World Café had 44 Rotary members (of the 56 members) attend, as well as two visiting Rotarian guests.

The data collected from the Prince Rupert Rotary Club focus group and World Café were sorted and compiled into key issues. Table 5 indicates the themes that arose from these key issues.

Table 5. *Key Themes from Prince Rupert Rotary Club Focus Group and World Café*

Topic	Key Issues	Themes
What Members Like about the Rotary Club	Give back to the community	Service
	Social aspects	Fellowship, Friendship
	International services and projects	International Service Learning
	Learn in a friendly environment	Fellowship, Friendship
Improve Member Participation	Good leadership	Leadership
	Good communication	Communication
	Involve everyone	Leadership, Fellowship, Friendship
	Rotation of members on committees	Fellowship, Friendship Learning
Members Wish Changed	Negative image	Communication
	Decline in membership	Membership
	New member orientation	Membership
	Ensure all committees function effectively	Leadership
	Burn out of members	Membership, Leadership
Value of Rotary	Makes a tangible difference in people's lives	Service Leadership
	Members are community leaders	Leadership Learning
	Is a safe place to be	

Topic	Key Issues	Themes
Selection of Funding Recipients	Process and criteria based on merit	Leadership
	Determine community benefits	Service
	Standardized application forms	Leadership
Public's Knowledge of Rotary	Generally unaware	Communication
	Those who know about Rotary are impressed	Communication
	Thought Rotary members were elitists	Communication
	Exclusive businessmen's club	Communication
Research Question: "How can the Rotary Club best expand its volunteer service to the community?"	Another major project needs common vision and values	Service
		Fellowship, Friendship
	Partnership with others	Partnership
	Avoid duplication of services	Leadership
	New member orientation process	Membership
	Gap Analysis of all services, which is a study to help organizations compare actual performance with potential performance	Service

Table 6. *Number of Times Each Theme Appeared in Prince Rupert Rotary Club Discussions during Focus Group and World Café*

	Number of Respondents
Theme	(*N* = 46)
Leadership	9
Communication	6

Fellowship and friendship	5
Service	5
Membership	4
Learning	3
Partnership	1
International service	1

All participants of the focus group and World Café were members of the Rotary Club and produced consistent answers to each of the questions. As well, participants could choose more than one answer.

The number of occurrences of the themes was in response to the questions asked (see Appendices G and J). The most-produced themes from the focus group and World Café with Rotarians included leadership, communication, fellowship and friendships, service, and membership.

Interpreting the focus group data required me to differentiate between "what participants found interesting and what they found important" (Morgan, 1997, p. 62). This was also applicable when interpreting the World Café data. According to Morgan,

> There are three basic factors that influence how much emphasis a given topic should receive: how many groups mentioned the topic, how many people within each of these groups mentioned the topic, and how much energy and enthusiasm the topic generated among the participants (p. 63).

I used Morgan's criteria to interpret the data from the focus group, and I compared the data to the World Café data to determine confirmation or disagreement of the information.

What Members like about Rotary

When focus group participants were asked what they liked most about Rotary, the majority of participants agreed it was to give back to the community, fellowship, friendship, and the social aspects. The majority of participants stated they also liked the opportunity to participate in international services and projects. The participants also indicated learning in a friendly environment was important. When participants of the World Café were asked what they liked most about Rotary, each table, at least once, identified the similar themes as the focus group. These themes were: community service, fellowship, friendship, and learning. All focus group participants stated they experienced fellowship and friendship though committees, fund-raising, Rotary Club events, and social gatherings. These key themes of giving back to the community, friendship, fellowship, social aspects, international projects, and learning emerged from both the focus group and the World Café.

The fellowship of the Rotary Club encourages members to improve themselves through participation and trying new activities. World Café participants liked the opportunity to learn and participate in self-improvement activities. They stated they learned from the variety of speakers at the meetings, the networking with other members and guests during lunch, and the various reports from the members. "Leaders in a culture of change create these conditions for daily learning, and they learn to lead by experiencing such learning at the hands of other leaders" (Fullan, 2001, p. 131). It was mentioned by many participants of both the focus group and the World Café that "Rotary is a safe place to be."

The majority of focus group participants mentioned that "Rotary was a place where one can practice skills such as public speaking, and gain knowledge to increase capacity to better serve the community as well as improve work skills." Kouzes and Posner (2002) stated, "Strengthening others requires that leaders provide a climate conducive to learning.…

Prime requirements for people to be capable of learning—changing and developing new skills—is that they feel safe" (p. 309).

"Many things can only be learned by interacting with other people, so social learning skills are most important. Also, the learning process is usually an experiential one, because the learning occurs while engaged in work projects" (Knowles, Holton, & Swanson, 2005, p. 319). As a result, all participants expressed their enjoyment of the friendly social aspects offered by club and the opportunity to participate in learning and training.

> There is much valuable experience gained from serving on a management committee or board. The range of management tasks undertaken, from strategic management to financial administration offers a type of experience which it can take years to gain through a job (Gann, 1996, p. 101).

These experiences, such as becoming a director or committee chair within the Rotary Club are readily available to any member who would like to become involved in various leadership roles.

As well as serving the local community, most focus group participants expressed the importance of having the opportunity to participate and contribute to international projects. These comments were supported by discussions at the World Café. As Rotary is a world-wide organization, there are opportunities to become involved in a myriad of international projects. These projects are offered through an arm of Rotary International (Rotary Foundation). The mission of The Rotary Foundation is to enable Rotarians "to advance world understanding, goodwill, and peace through the improvement of health, the support of education, and the alleviation of poverty" (Rotary International, 2007c, ¶ 12). The Foundation offers education programs in which Rotarians can participate, such as ambassadorial scholarships, group study exchange, Rotary grants for university teachers, the Rotary peace and conflict studies program, and the Rotary world peace fellowships, to name just a few of the program(¶ 6–10).

Furthermore, locally supported international projects are partnered with third world clubs and District Clubs who wish to participate. These Rotary Clubs completed a clean water projects in Ginir, Ethiopia, and fund-raised for the polio plus campaign to eradicate polio in the world. Without Rotary International, participation in international projects can be limited. Members appreciate and value the opportunity to serve the community as well as the third world countries (Rotary

International, 2007c, ¶ 6–10). The funds raised for international projects are received from the members and the supporters of Rotary and not from locally-sponsored fund-raisers.

Improving Members' Participation

Members participate in club activities to raise funds and provide services for various service projects. Rotary Club provides the opportunities for members to serve in a variety of capacities through their appointment to various committees that perform a variety of services. The members are appointed to a committee annually prior to the beginning of the Rotary year, July first. When participants were asked about the current appointment process, many participants suggested there needs to be a timely rotation of member appointments to various committees. The reason for members to be appointed to different committees is to ensure members remain interested and committed. Committees allow members to work and serve with a variety of people outside their daily life. This offers them the opportunity to make new friends and experience fellowship with others. Ilsley (1990) asked, "How can an organization motivate volunteers not only to join the organization but to stay with it? Clearly the organization needs to build flexibility into its program—allowing volunteer to change tasks and roles" (p. 31).

Six focus group participants commented they believed that some committees were not functioning well. These participants stated there needs to be effective communication to ensure all committee members are included and involved. There were four World Café participants who also expressed concern regarding ineffective committees.

It was stated that "real consideration must be given to who is put on what committee and what are the terms of reference" (Focus Group Participant #1). "The selection of members to the committees was very important and influenced the success of the committee" (Focus Group Participant #2). The majority of focus group participants expressed their opinion that good leadership by the President and committee chairs has a big influence on member participation. "Leadership, communication, and inclusiveness of all members will improve member participation within the club structure" (Focus Group Participant #4). Members' participation on committees, in activities, and service projects was seen to be important to the well being of the club and the members.

Therefore, participants felt it was very important the Rotary Club strategize to achieve greater member participation in Rotary activities.

Changes Members Wanted to See in the Rotary Club

The committees are established to ensure inclusive, effective, and appropriate services of members in the activities of the club. All focus group participants expressed the need for committees to function effectively and efficiently. There was strong concern about the ineffectiveness of some of the committees, thereby, causing some members to lose interest. "A committee meeting that does not make any decisions about where it is going destroys that committee" (Focus Group Participant #5). Another related comment was: "Decisions not being asked for by committees are deadly. Members do not want their time wasted by committees that do not function well" (Focus Group Participant #5). These concerns were confirmed by comments from the World Café. As stated by Wolf (1999), "Committee meetings, like board meetings, should have tight agendas and should not waste people's time" (p. 72). However, effective committees are very important to the organizations, as expressed by Wolf:

A committee structure has several advantages. First, it allows for a division of the workload. Second, it promotes a more informal discussion of the pros and cons of various issues before they come to the board for a formal resolution. Third, it allows an organization to bring experts into the deliberation process without putting them on the board (pp. 69–70).

Participants in both the focus group and World Café felt that appointments to committees are an excellent way to initiate new members, giving them the opportunity to become familiar with the club. New members add to the ability for the membership to perform the services to the community, which adds the tremendous value of Rotary. Without new members, the "current members get burned out by trying to do too much" (Focus Group Participant #8). This issue was also identified in the World Café. The most important criteria for a success committee are the evaluation process. The Rotary Club needs to evaluate what the committees are doing well and where committees are not functioning effectively and implement an action plan to achieve success of all committees.

Another response from both the focus group and World Café participants identified the decline in Rotary membership. Membership decline was a concern of all the focus group participants and all the groups of the World Café confirmed this concern.

The Rotary Club needs to be an organization that people would want to join and belong. Several participants of both focus group and World Café identified a perception by the public that viewed Rotary as an elitist club, a businessmen's club, or an exclusive club not welcoming to the general public to consider or want to join. This opinion was made by all participants of Focus Group #1 and mentioned numerous times during the World Café. This perception may not be true, but is an undesirable element of public image. Therefore, Rotarians agreed it was important to strive to change the present club image, as the members did not view themselves as elitist or exclusive. The way to change the public image of the Rotary Club is to make the value of Rotary known to the community. Another change the members wished was for effective and active committees that encouraged all members to be involved.

Value of Rotary

The value of Rotary is the "services to the community that makes the difference in peoples lives" (Focus Group Participant #1). This value was also stated by World Café participants. Stebbins and Graham (2004) defined leisure volunteering as:

> social capital that constitutes an enormous reservoir of skills, energy, and local and special interest knowledge. Volunteering as leisure gives participants a sense of purpose, provokes serious contemplation, encourages concern for others, provides the opportunity to further an interest, and to have fun and enjoyment (p. 241).

Rotarians have been identified as community leaders by both members and the community. "As community leaders, we can share the value of Rotary with those less fortunate" (Focus Group Participant # 7).

The participants of both focus group and World Café stated another value of Rotary is the opportunity for members to learn in a friendly environment. The participants expressed the members can learn such skills a public speaking, running of meetings, gleaning information from speakers, and interacting with other members from various vocations. Therefore, the value of Rotary is twofold, one is the service to the community and the other is the service to its members.

Public Knowledge of Rotary

The data from the focus group, the World Café, interviews, and surveys confirmed the Rotary Club serves the community well, but the public generally is not very aware of Rotary. Public knowledge of the Rotary Club is beneficial, as it can encourage people to be interested in joining the Rotary Club. This opinion was shared by both the Rotary members and the community members interviewed and surveyed. However, it was agreed by the all participants of the two focus groups, the majority of the World Café, one-on-one interviews, and surveys from the service provider organizations, that the people who knew about Rotary, highly respected and appreciated the work that Rotary does for the community. This statement is supported by the Official Community Plan of the City of Prince Rupert (2007), which stated the community as a whole felt that service organizations such as Rotary were one of the dimensions of community life that is performing well.

It is imperative that Rotary increase its public profile, to entice new members to join and to get the community to know about the Rotary Club and realize the value of Rotary to the community. Focus group participants stated that Rotary is not known to the people of the community, even considering the amount of services and projects done by Rotary members. World Café participants confirmed the opinion the public is not aware of what the Rotary Club does for the community.

Expanding the Rotary Club's Volunteer Services to the Community

The majority of the public may not be aware of the work of the Rotary Club in the community. However, service to the community was frequently stated by the participants of both focus groups and the World Café as very important to the members. Several participants expressed the Rotary Club needs to establish another community major service project to enable the members the opportunity to become involved. The majority of participants stated it was also important that members within the club share the same vision and values in selecting a major project. "Unless the majority of the members support the major project, that project can fail" (Focus Group Participant #4).

A major service project requires a very large amount of money and takes up a lot of members' time and energies. Services to the youth were mentioned as a potential major service project. However, it was generally agreed the Hecate Strait Rotary Club focused on youth and that the Rotary Club (Rotary Club of Prince Rupert) should not take over what is already being done. Participants expressed their desire to help both the gifted youth, as well as the problem youth. The Rotary Club members also stated that partnerships with other organizations and with the Hecate Strait Rotary Club were very important. By working together, the services to the community will not be duplicated and can be greatly enhanced.

Cooperation between Both Rotary Clubs in Prince Rupert Using Focus Group

Services to the community can be better served by both clubs working together and planning together. In discussions held with both Club members and the community, the subject of partnerships and working together surfaced frequently. The focus group discussions that were held with the Hecate Strait Rotary Club proved to be very informative and helpful to my research questions: "How can the Rotary Club of Prince Rupert best expand its volunteer services to the community?"

The Hecate Strait Rotary Club focus group was attended by 18 of its 27 members and two visiting Rotarians. One Rotarian declined to sign the consent form (see Appendix D) and was advised that he was very welcome to stay, although I could not use any comments he made, as I did not have his consent to use that information. I observed that this member did not participate in any of the discussions. The key issues that arose from the meeting with the Hecate Strait Rotary Club are summarized in Table 7.

Table 7. *Key Themes from Focus Group with Hecate Strait Rotary Club*

Topic	Key Issues	Themes
How the Two Rotary Clubs Can Work Together	Have regular joint committee meetings	Leadership Communication Partnership
	Both clubs to meet at least twice during the year and one time prior to President-Elect Training Seminar (PETS)	Leadership Communication Partnership
	Both clubs to meet at least twice during the year and one time prior to President-Elect Training Seminar (PETS)	Leadership Communication Partnership
	Dual executive meetings in September and again in March	Leadership Communication Partnership
Joint Projects and Services	Presidents to meet prior to PETS and plan the year	Leadership Communication Partnership International service Partnership
	International and district projects	Partnership Service
	Hands on projects	Partnership Service
	Youth issues	Partnership Leadership
	Promote Rotary to youths	

Topic	Key Issues	Themes
Research Question: "How can the Rotary Club best expand its volunteer service to the community?"	Increase Rotary awareness in community	Communication
	Coordinate service organizations to avoid duplication of services	Leadership Partnership Communication
	Shed businessmen's image	Communication

Table 8. *Number of Times Each Theme Appeared in Focus Group with Hecate Strait Rotary Club*

Theme	Number of Respondents (N = 18)
Partnership	10
Communication	8
Leadership	7
Service	2
International service	1
Fellowship and friendship	0
Learning	0
Membership	0

The information from the second focus group was conducted by open forum and participants could chose more than one answer. The focus group questions (see Appendix M) were specifically designed for the Hecate Strait Rotary Club to focus on how the two clubs can work effectively together. The questions asked during the meeting (see Appendix M), and the answers were recorded by one of their members on a poster board on the wall. At the conclusion of the focus group, I reviewed the comments with the participants at the meeting and inquired if the comments captured their views or if any comment did not belong. All participants agreed the information accurately reflected their views. Following the focus group, an email was sent to all participants that contained a summary of the discussions for their comment and corrections. Five responses were received, and all concurred with the summary.

To establish common goals and long-term plans, participants of the second Focus Group suggested the "President-elects of both clubs should meet immediately after President Elects Training Seminar (PETS) held annual specifically for leadership training. This training session is held in Seattle Washington, every year in February or March. This will ensure that the President-elects can work together to plan their year as President, which will commence on July 1" (Focus Group Participant #2). Participants further commented that the Board of Directors of both clubs should meet once or twice a year to set plans and priorities and follow up to ensure the two clubs are meeting and productively planning.

Productive planning of activities for both Rotary Clubs would include joint projects, such as international projects and local youth services. "This can be as basic as promoting Rotary to youths so they can see and learn what community leaders do to serve the community (Focus Group Participant #2). Rotary awareness should also be expanded to include the community, and when people became more familiar with Rotary, participants believed the image of businessmen's club can be eliminated.

The improvement of Rotary's image in the community will entice the public's interest and support of Rotary's role in the community. Participants believed that Rotary can assist organizations to work together for the common good and avoid duplication of services. This concurred with the comments from the first Focus Group that a Gap Analysis of the community needs and concerns would have great value for Rotary to plan its community services. Morgan (1997) stated, "The key defining feature of self contained focus group is the ability to report the data from focus groups as a sufficient body of knowledge" (p. 21). Therefore, the information was used as the basis for my research report on how the Rotary Club can work in partnership with the Hecate Strait Rotary Club.

The themes communication, leadership, and partnerships evolved, and participants stated strengthening leadership and communication would contribute to the two Rotary Clubs working effectively together. This sharing of information should be used to establish mutual common goals and long term plans. In addition to the information gathered from the Hecate Strait Rotary Club, it was also necessary to obtain information from those outside of Rotary to achieve another perspective.

Community's Perspectives Using Interviews and Surveys

The community perspective was obtained through interviews with the members of City Council. All members of the City council were invited to attend. Of the seven council members, four councillors participated. Three senior staff were invited to participate and all three attended.

A survey was used to obtain information from the service provider organizations. Fifteen service provider organizations were sent the survey, and 11 completed surveys were received. Forty members of the public were randomly selected and were sent the survey but no responses were received. To ensure consistency of data, the research questions for the interviews (see Appendix L) and surveys (see Appendix O) were kept similar to the focus group sessions (see Appendices G and M) and the World Café questions (see Appendix J). The data from both the interviews and the survey were then sorted and compiled to highlight common areas of discussions among all participants.

The themes that arose are summarized in Table 9.

Table 9. *Key Themes from the Interviews and Survey*

Topic	Comments	Themes
What You Perceive the Members like about the Rotary Club	Give back to the community	Service
	Social aspects	Fellowship, Friendship
	A sense of belonging	Fellowship, Friendship
Public's Knowledge of the Rotary Club	Generally unaware	Communication
	Those who know about Rotary are impressed	Communication
	Not a high profile	Communication
	Perception Rotary is a businessperson's club	Communication

Topic	Comments	Themes
Value of Rotary	Is the connection to the community	Leadership
	Members are community leaders	Leadership
	Encourages other people to get involved in community service	Leadership
Selection of Funding to Recipients	Established process and criteria based on merit	Leadership
	Align with community objectives	Leadership
	Proposals that take away bias and meet the criteria	Communication
	Projects that enhance the city.	Service
	Projects based on criteria and community needs	Service
Rotary Club's Assistance to City Hall	Joint projects	Partnership
	To bring service groups	Leadership
	together to strategize activities and projects.	Partnership
	City to have a five-year plan and bring Rotary and other service groups to do the plan	Leadership
		Service
Expansion of the Rotary Club's Volunteer Services to the Community	Stable volunteer base	Leadership
	Youths need a champion to share leadership skills with them	Leadership
	Rotary is a leading organization	Leadership
	Provide training in leadership	Leadership

Table 10. *Number of Times each Theme Appeared in Interviews and Survey*

	Number of Respondents
Theme	($N = 46$)
Leadership	11
Communication	5
Service	4
Partnership	2
Fellowship and friendship	2
International service	0
Learning	0
Membership	0

The themes most mentioned are leadership, communication, service, and partnership. This result is appropriate as the information was from the community participants. Study findings also revealed similarities of the value of Rotary to the community between the Rotary members and the community. The key issue of the public's lack of knowledge of Rotary was again mentioned by the interviews and surveys. However, all interview and survey participants were very knowledgeable about the community as well as Rotary. The community participants believed that people join Rotary to be able to give back to the community. They also agreed with Rotary members that the general public is not very aware of Rotary, and those who know about Rotary are very impressed with the work and services that Rotary provides.

Rotary Club's Assistance to City Hall

The services and work of Rotary are viewed by City Hall and service provider organizations as a valuable asset to the community. As my research evolved, the majority of participants, through both the interview and the survey expressed the Rotary Club and the city could benefit from joint participation in services to the community. All interview participants identified there could be joint participation whereby the Rotary Club could initiate working with the staff at City Hall, as each share a common interest in community improvement projects. It was suggested by all interview participants that the Rotary Club and City Hall need to discuss matters of mutual interest prior to projects being initiated, to ensure that both the Rotary Club and the city coordinate the efforts.

The example given was the city's major focus to assist with youth violence situations. All interview participants viewed Rotarians as community leaders who can take a major role of influence with this issue. The majority of interview participants also expressed the desire for Rotary to coordinate the activities of various organizations that provide similar youth services to the community.

Working in cooperation with City Hall and the service provider organizations, the majority of participants believed that the Rotary Club could be the driving force to contribute to the success of projects. The majority of interview participants believed that the involvement of the Rotary Club gave community projects the credibility needed to succeed. They further commented that Rotary serves as a good example for other organizations. Therefore, there is a major role for Rotary to partner with these organizations to coordinate the services in the community. There were numerous concerns regarding duplication of services by many organizations in the community. It was stated that "Rotary can participate to improve social and economic well being and can achieve this goal by partnerships with these organizations and the city to co-ordinate the community services" (Survey Participant #1).

Expanding the Rotary Club's Volunteer Services to Community

The Rotary Club, through partnerships with the City Hall and service provider organizations, can offer valuable leadership and participation. All interview participants were very knowledgeable of the services of Rotary. In response to the questions asked (see Appendices L and O), the majority of city and service provider participants expressed similar opinions that they would like to see the Rotary Club participate in services to the troubled youth. All City Hall participants believed that the Rotary Club does an exceptional service to gifted youth in their various student programs. These programs are where an exchange student would be sent to another country for a year, and one student form another country would come to live in this community to learn our culture and ways of living. These exchange students would be the responsibility of the sponsoring Rotary Club. It is the purpose of the student exchange programme to bring peace and understanding amongst various countries throughout the world.

Rotary also supports academic students who excel in leadership through their participation in various citizenship programs, such as Rotary Youth Leadership Training (Rotary International, 2007h,

¶ 1–2). Eight scholarships from the two Rotary Clubs are awarded annually to students advancing to post secondary education in either the technical or academic area of study. As well as supporting gifted youths, the majority of participants believed that the Rotary Club should also be involved with helping the troubled youths. "There are so many disadvantaged youths in our community who are fighting the culture of poverty and do not know how to move away from this state" (Interview Participant #1). "There are youths who are not engaged and needs opportunities to learn and Rotarians as leaders of the community can set a good example for them to follow" (Interview Participant #3). "Youths need a champion to share leadership skills with them so they can learn to be leaders" (Interview Participant #1).

As well as services to youths, the majority of interview and survey participants stated the need in the community to participate in health services, senior citizens issues, and home support. "Improved recreational services and opportunities for youths, seniors, and underprivileged would address health concerns for many people, as well as the youth, seniors, and the underprivileged families" (Survey Participant #4).

Currently, there are organizations whose mandate is to look after the socially disadvantaged as well as other community services, but it was felt by several community participants that Rotary can play a major role in bringing service groups together to strategize activities, services, and projects. There was concern regarding duplication of services amongst organizations, which caused them to work against one another primarily for funds, whereas working together would benefit the under-privileged. It was mentioned several times by survey and interview participants that Rotary can initiate partnerships by formalizing joint participation.

Study Conclusions

The research study reviewed the information from the perspective of the members, the organization, and the community. This information was obtained from focus groups, World Café, one-on-one interviews, and surveys. The data analysis identified the key themes, which were supported by the literature reviewed, and enabled me to answer the research question: "How can the Rotary Club of Prince Rupert best expand its volunteer services to the community?" The main themes identified by all meetings of the focus groups, World Café, interviews, and surveys revealed the needs of both the members and the community. These main themes identified the benefits of being a member as giving back to the community, friendship, fellowship, social aspects to get to know a variety of people, and learning for self-improvement. The members' concerns were that not all members participate in the various club activities and events. It was stated there is a challenge to the club to determine how to get more members to participate and to contribute their time and expertise. As Dekker and Halman (2003) questioned, "Why do people volunteer? One explanation could be that volunteering reflects a person's personality: some people are by nature helpful, active and generous, and some people are less so" (p. 3). They further surmised,

> We probably all know those people who always do something extra, are always willing to help, ready to take the initiative, whether in the workplace, in the neighbourhood, or at home. And we also know the other kind of people who remain passive most of the time, always having something else to do, are too tired (p. 3).

It was stated by all participants that the many services and funds that active members give to the community did not result in making

Rotary known to the public. Participants generally believed that those who know about Rotary admire, respect, and appreciate members' contributions with no expectation of anything in return. The comments from both focus group and the World Café participants concurred the public does not know very much about Rotary; there was the perception that members were elitist—a businessmen's club or exclusive. The members appear committed to changing this image of Rotary.

The public opinions influence the Rotary Club's ability to attract new members, a very high priority for the Rotary Club. Once new members joined the club, members wished to have better new member orientation. New member orientation would be to share the knowledge of Rotary service, the history of Rotary, and the value of Rotary, which will entice the new members to become committed to the Rotary Club. Keeping volunteers motivated and helping their motivations to evolve in positive directions, Ilsley (1990) suggested, "Soon after volunteers join the organization, work out explicit agreements that specify a feasible commitment of time and other resources and allow for personal variations in time, energy, and interest" (p. 32).

The Hecate Strait Rotary Club focus group identified the need for the two clubs to work together for the benefit of the community. Participants suggested having regular joint meetings of their respective committees. It was further suggested that both clubs meet at lease twice during the year and the executive members of each club meet in September and again in March to ensure that stated goals and objectives are being met. Participants further suggested that each President-elect meet to plan their year as President before attending President-Elects Training Seminar (PETS), which is generally held in February or March. Once becoming President, it was stated they meet in six months time to evaluate their plans to work together. As well, participants wished to work together on international and district projects, improve the image of Rotary, and increase Rotary awareness in the community.

The interviews with City Hall and surveys from the service provider organizations identified the need for groups and organizations to work together for the benefit of the community and the organizations. The participants further stated the need for partnerships with organizations to initiate a plan to coordinate community services to eliminate duplication of these services. The interview participants expressed the desire for the Rotary Club to work with the city to establish a five-year plan for community services that involved volunteer service organizations.

The Rotary Club partnering with the Hecate Strait Rotary Club, the City Hall, and service provider organizations requires good leadership and communication to achieve the objectives of working together and establishing partnerships. The study findings indicated leadership and communication were major themes from focus groups, World Café, interviews, and surveys.

This research study was extensive and endeavoured to obtain input from all those concerned and affected by this community-based action research. The input was provided by 44 members representing the Rotary Club, 17 members from the Hecate Strait Club and 15 participants representing the community (see Table 1).

Scope and Limitations of Research

The scope of this research, as stated by Ilsley (1990), "do[es] not claim to have sampled the entire spectrum of formal volunteer organizations, but we believe that we surveyed a wide enough variety to uncover similarities and differences that are both significant and accurate" (p. 151).

Leedy and Ormrod (2005) cautioned that "when formulating conclusions about the data, a researcher must be sure to consider the effect that bias may have had in distorting them" (p. 210). They further stated,

> Good researchers demonstrate their integrity by admitting, without reserve, that bias is omnipresent and may well have influenced their findings. Ideally, they point out precisely how bias may have infiltrated the research design. With this knowledge, others may then appraise the research realistically and judge its merits honestly (p. 210).

Therefore, readers are cautioned that the data collected from the members of both Rotary Clubs may not be representative of the general membership of other Rotary Clubs. Furthermore, data collected from the city councillors and the service provider organizations will vary from community to community, depending on various factors such as economics, demographics, social and cultural beliefs, and age factors.

Because of the varying factors, not only of communities but of organizations, the limitations of the study of volunteer organizations, leadership, and the motives for volunteering are endless. I have performed this research project primarily for the benefit of the members of the Rotary Club. Studying about Rotary is also an extensive endeavour, as there are so many facets of Rotary that were out of scope of this research study. Interpreting the data required skills, objectivity, and understanding. The challenge stated by Denzin (1989) addressed "understanding the process of interpreting, knowing, and comprehending the meaning that is felt, intended and expressed by another" (p. 120). To add to this, "different minds often find different meaning in the same set of facts" (Leedy & Ormrod, 2005, p. 6). As a Rotarian, my knowledge of Rotary could influence my understanding of the various components of Rotary service. Therefore, it is imperative that I discuss my assumptions to ensure the readers are aware of them and how they would read my study based on their assumptions.

Leedy and Ormrod, (2005) reminded me that the "careful researcher state their assumptions so that others inspecting the research project may evaluate it in accordance with their own assumptions" (p. 5). Therefore, to follow Leedy and Ormrod's advice, my assumptions are the Rotary Club: (a) exists to provide community service; (b) gives its members the opportunity to participate in volunteer service; (c) does not discriminate against race, religion, political affiliations, and other prejudices; (d) does not exist for the personal gain of its members; and (e) acknowledges that everyone is different and members accept each other because of their differences.

> Booth et al. (2003) stated, Readers judge a writer but a thoughtful writer has in advance also judged her readers by imagining who they are, what they are, what they know, what they need and want. And then she uses that judgement to shape what she writes (p. 18).

Through this community-based action research study, I collected and analyzed data and information to produce the evidence for the conclusions based on the study findings. The key issues identified by all research methods concluded Rotary is a valued organization that serves its members and provides valuable services locally and internationally, but needs to look at partnerships with other organizations, increase its awareness within the community, and provide services to youth and projects that make the community better.

Based on my assumptions and knowledge of Rotary and the data I have collected from the members of the club and the community, the research study indicates the need for change within the Rotary Club. This data and information collected have been analysed and triangulated to ensure validity and trustworthiness of the data. This data produced evidence for the conclusions, based on this community-based action research project's study findings and supported by the review of the literature of academic authors.

The study findings indicate change is necessary, if the Rotary Club is to meet the needs of the members and the community by becoming an effective organization today and into the future. The change requires good communication and leadership that will entice participation of the members and retain the current members while enticing new members to join.

This research study has been prepared as a thesis submitted in partial fulfillment of the requirements for the degree of Master of Arts in Leadership & Training from the Royal Roads University (2006). My research question was, "How can the Rotary Club of Prince Rupert best expand its volunteer services to the community?" Therefore, this study has been written to assist the Rotary Club of Prince Rupert in its endeavours to be a viable, effective, and valuable organization serving the community and its members. It is also hoped that this research study would be of value to other Rotary Clubs, as well as community volunteer organizations. The organizational changes required to implement the recommendations are discussed in Chapter Five.

CHAPTER FIVE: RESEARCH IMPLICATIONS

Through this community-based action research project, I identified the research findings, themes, and conclusions, which formed the basis for my recommendations. I have outlined the process for implementing these recommendations to enable the changes required within the Rotary Club to best expand its volunteer services to the community. The project recommendations discuss the members' needs and expectations, the need to identify the organization's goals and objectives, and how to meet the needs of the community.

The recommendations are discussed in the following sub-topic: (a) leadership and communication: good leaders, good communicators; (b) service: give back to the community; (c) service: international projects; (s) social aspects; fellowships and friendships; (e) membership: new members, long-time members, and their participation; (f) learning and training: Rotary is a safe place; (g) partnerships: to build stronger communities and organizations; and (h) public relations: public does not know. Each sub-topic states the recommended actions required to address these key themes identified by the participants of focus groups, word café, interviews, and surveys.

Project Recommendations

In compiling the project recommendations, I have reviewed the data obtained from the focus groups, World Café, interviews, and surveys, discussed them in detail, and explained the recommendations for each topic. The questions presented to the participants provided the catalyst to find the answers to my research questions and produce the relevant recommendations.

I used the community-based action research process to find the answers to my research question, which involved participants examining their own needs, beliefs, and expectations to assess their role in the organization. The project recommendations resulted from reviewing findings from the perspective of the members of Rotary Clubs, the organization, and the community. These findings have been applied to identify the answers to my research question: "How can the Rotary Club of Prince Rupert best expand its volunteer services to the community?"

Nancy Eidsvik, MA

Leadership and Communication: Good Leaders, Good Communicators

It is recommended the Rotary Club provides leadership training for all members appointed as President, President-elect, secretary, treasurer, and directors. This training can be done through Rotary Leadership Institute training (Rotary District 5040, 2007c, ¶ 1–7), attendance at district assembly (Rotary District 5040, 2007a, ¶ 1–4), and other Rotary training seminars. It is imperative to elect and appoint members who are effective leaders—committed, knowledgeable, and appropriate for the responsibilities that have been entrusted to them. Good leaders know the "importance of modeling the behaviour that you want to encourage in others" (Parks, 2005, p. 113). Therefore, a good leader will attend all the required meetings as possible, and is reliable, responsible and sincere. Good leaders are not ones who do things themselves, but have the "ability to give the work back to the group so that it can learn and adapt to make progress on our toughest challenges" (p. 256).

"Creative leaders highly value individuality. They sense that people perform at a higher level when they are operating on the basis of their unique strengths, talents, interests, and goals than when they are trying to conform to some imposed stereotype" (Knowles et al., 2005, p. 259). Good leaders encourage members to be themselves and respect them for who they are, not what the leader wants them to be.

> In contrast, Bacharach (2005) defined, Politically competent leaders do their up front homework to map the political terrain, understand who is likely to be on their side and who is likely to resist them. They get people on board and build a coalition. Then, they lead the coalition to get the results (p. 222).

I would recommend the Rotary Club avoid this type of political leadership and be aware of control of the organization by a few people.

Good leaders communicate both ways—to listen and then to be heard. Drucker (1990) stated, "As the first such basic competence, I would put the willingness, ability, and self-discipline to listen. Listening is not a skill; it's a discipline" (p. 20). Drucker further stated that the second the essential competence of the leader is the "willingness to communicate, to make yourself understood" (p. 20). Knowles et al. (2005) defined communication as having "open flow and easy access, is multidirectional—up, down, and sideways" (p/ 112).

Good leaders and their leadership are about helping the members to achieve their goals and needs. Good leadership welcomes open and honest communication that shares knowledge of activities and events with members to ensure they are informed and included. Good leadership begets good members—members who are happy, committed, and eager to serve.

Service: Give Back to the Community

It was identified through this research study that members joined Rotary for the opportunity to give back to the community. It is recommended that the Rotary Club ensures all members have the opportunity to participate and achieve positive experiences through their community service activities. It is imperative that the Rotary Club maintains its ability to provide community service. Without community service, the members will not have the opportunity to serve, to participate, and to enjoy the fellowship of the Rotary Club. These opportunities to serve arise from the projects undertaken by the Rotary Club.

The projects committee reviews and recommends the projects to the Board of Directors, who in turn recommends the project to the membership. It is important that members are encouraged to comment on these projects. "If your organization is going to be the best it can be, everyone has to feel comfortable in speaking up and taking the initiative" (Kouzes & Posner, 2002, p. 200).

It is imperative the projects committee functions effectively and decisions are made by projects committee members who are knowledgeable and informed. It must be the responsibility of the Board of Directors to ensure accountability and effectiveness of all committees. There needs to be written terms of reference for the projects committee and established, unbiased processes for the selection of funding applicants. It is further recommended to establish an evaluation process to measure success and effectiveness of the funds distributed.

These funds as approved are then distributed to various organizations or groups within the community. Therefore, it is important that a fair and equitable process for the selection of funding be established. It must be seen by the public that it is fair and unbiased. It is important to have a simple and consistent application process. As the funding is a function of the projects committee, it is necessary that this committee functions effectively, meets regularly, and the members are given the complete information to enable them to make good decisions.

Service: International Projects

It is recommended the Foundation Committee's mandate be expanded to consider and review all matters pertaining to other countries and report regularly to the members and the directors. This will ensure members are knowledgeable of international projects and third world issues.

Currently the only function of the Foundation Committee is to organize the annual fund-raising event for international projects. Funds raised from the local community are not put into projects outside of the community.

The study identified that members liked the opportunity to participate in international service through Rotary International. It is imperative the Board of Directors ensure the members are given the opportunity to participate in International projects. The opportunities for international service are abundant, and since the Rotary Club is affiliated with Rotary International, the only limitations for participation are influenced by the leadership and their decisions as to what projects to support.

Social Aspects: Fellowships and Friendships

The members also expressed the desire for fellowship, friendship, and social activities. The Rotary Club needs to focus on activities that provide these experiences for the members by ensuring an active and effective fellowship committee to organize club fellowship activities. It is equally important the Board of Directors maintain opportunities for members to participate in active and effective committees. Participation on committees gives members the social aspects that promote fellowships and friendships.

Another fellowship opportunity is the weekly noon meetings. It is imperative that these meetings are structured and presented in the way that members can have time to have conversations and develop friendships.

Nancy Eidsvik, MA

Membership: New Members, Longtime Members, and Their Participation

It is recommended the Rotary Club identify the reasons people join and stay members—as well as why members leave—to better meet the members' needs. It is recommended that every new member be given a questionnaire inquiring as to their interests, their expectations, how they wish to participate, and why they joined the Rotary Club.

A further recommendation is to implement an exit survey of all members who leave the club. This would be an opportunity to inquire as to the reason for their leaving and what the Rotary Club could have done differently to have enticed them to stay. It is imperative the knowledge why members joined Rotary is kept as a priority for the organization and is applied regularly in its functions and deliberations. One of the major considerations of the Rotary Club is to meet members' needs and expectations. It is the happy, committed member who will contribute time, money, and expertise to volunteer. Therefore, the retention of members is important to the organization.

> Ilsley (1990) stated volunteer managers can respect the values that lie behind commitment and recognize that those values, along with the commitment that springs from them, may

change during the cause of volunteers' work. By doing these things, they can design programs that draw on the volunteers' commitment (p. 56).

Without understanding the volunteer, the organization can lose its members. The organization needs members to maintain its abilities to provide fellowship activities, raise funds, or provide services to the community. Therefore, it is necessary that the Rotary Club leaders be cognizant of the reasons why people joined Rotary and how to keep the members happy, committed, and motivated to remain in the club.

This research study identified that the Rotary Club endeavours to provide these opportunities for all members. However, the study revealed a definite concern by members that not all members participate in club functions and committees. It is important to acknowledge that not all members want to participate in all events. To evaluate member participation, it is important the leaders of the organization have an accurate record of member participation and ensure this is not determined arbitrarily by feel and impressions.

Members can readily be discouraged if leaders give them the impression that they are not contributing to the welfare of the club, when in reality they really are. Hybels (2004) described a volunteer who "worked hard on menial tasks without ever hearing how their efforts served a grander cause" (p. 25). He further gave another example that "many have been hurt when a coercive leader drafted them to 'fill a slot' without considering their gifts or talents or what they love to do" (p. 25). Leaders need to be sensitive and aware of what their members are doing and perhaps going unnoticed. "Others have fled overwhelmed by unreasonable demands for which they've not received proper training, rather than being set up to win, they get put on the express lane to frustration and failure" (p. 25).

Learning and Training: Rotary is a Safe Place

It is recommended the Rotary Club hold "fireside" events for new-member orientation at least twice a year. A fireside is a meeting generally held in a member's home, whereby discussions are held regarding all aspects of Rotary including membership requirements, attendance requirements, Rotary Foundation, fund-raising, and all other general information. It is further recommended that all members be encouraged to attend (a) district training sessions, (b) district assemblies, and (c) district and world Rotary conventions. It is further recommended the Rotary Club establish a budget for the purpose of member training and financial assistance to attend out-of-town conventions and training sessions.

It is also recommended that a mentoring programme be developed and initiated. This programme will ensure new members are taught about Rotary to obtain interest and commitment from the new members. Palmer (1998) stated, "Mentors and apprentices are partners as the old empower the young with their experience and the young empower the old with new life" (p. 25).

Participants stated the Rotary Club makes a difference in the lives of people. Members believed that Rotary is a safe place to be and gives them opportunities to learn new skills, try different activities, and participate in fellowship without fear of discrimination or being judged. It is necessary for the Rotary Club to continue to provide opportunities for the members to learn and participate in a safe place.

Another form of learning was described by Senge (2006) as "learning in this context, does not mean acquiring more information, but expanding the ability to produce the results we truly want in life" (p. 132). The Rotary Club must offer a variety of experiences, challenging activities, and enjoyable fellowship to add to the learning of the members.

Training and participation are paramount in retaining new members. However, leaders need to consider that sometimes new members can be overwhelmed with the amount of duties they are expected to do. "Long time volunteer can handle an occasional volunteer mishap. But a new volunteer is extremely vulnerable to discouragement and disillusionment" (Hybels, 2004 p. 113). It takes a good leader to know when there is too much involvement and expectation of the volunteer and not enough.

Partnerships: To Build Stronger Communities and Organizations

Hecate Strait Rotary Club

It is recommended the two Rotary Clubs hold executive meetings of both clubs in September to establish the year's goals and meet again in March, to ensure clubs are on target as to the goals and objectives. It is further recommended the President-elects meet prior to President-Elects Training Seminar (PETS) in February to set goals and objectives, and then meet again in September to ensure the plans are in place.

As a joint project, the participants wished to promote youth issues. It was determined by participants that communication would be the answer to the two clubs working effectively. The joint meetings and joint projects would do much to build partnerships in service to the community.

Once the schedules for meetings are established, it is imperative that the Board of Directors ensure that these meetings are held and their members attend and participate. It is important for leaders to accept their responsibilities of being directors and to ensure they perform their duties actively and consistently. There needs to be an evaluation process established that ensure these timelines and meetings are being met and acted upon. Without the evaluation process, the members of both Rotary Clubs will lose interest and will not remain committed.

Projects for the two Rotary Clubs that would serve the community were identified as services to the youth, partnerships with other organizations, and projects that make the community better. Members said a Gap Analysis of community services was necessary to obtain all the pertinent information to assist the Rotary Club to address these issues.

City Hall

Participants from City Hall have expressed the desire to implement a partnership with the Rotary Club to identify services to troubled youths. City Hall interview participants stated Rotary is the organization that can get things done in the city and ensure the projects are completed. However, City Hall would like the Rotary Club to communicate with their staff prior to a project being undertaken to ensure the project does fit within their scope and plans. It is evident communication is the key in assisting City Hall.

As well, the Rotary Club participants identified services to the youth as very worthy causes. It is important that the Rotary Club ensures there is sufficient knowledge and information regarding youth in Prince Rupert before making decisions. Therefore, it is recommended that further studies be done on identifying the services to the youth, what services already exist, and what organizations are involved.

The Gap Analysis or a needs assessment is an excellent means to identify community needs and also what exists and what is missing. This type of information gathering is very valuable. Projects that make the community better will evolve when the studies and data gathering have been achieved. The answers will be in the further research study.

Public Relations: Public Is Not Aware

To address the issue of negative image due to the public not knowing what the Rotary Club does, it is recommended that a Public Relations Committee be enacted and mandated to perform its duties in a timely and effective manner. The participants of both focus groups and World Café identified the need for improved public relations as the public was unaware of Rotary and the services it provides. This also resulted in the incorrect image the public has that the club projects elitism, a business men's club, and an organization that is exclusive. However, the members did not see themselves as elite, a businessmen's club, or exclusive. The way to counter this image is by better and effective public relations to convey the message of Rotary to the community.

The participants of the Hecate Strait Rotary Club focus group identified the need to increase Rotary awareness in the community. They also expressed the desire to shed business men's club image. This image will limit enticing new members to join.

The public relations committee must develop a strategy of goals and objectives to improve the image of the Rotary Club, including how to publicize the good work in the community. The Board of Directors need to measure the achievement of these goals on a timely basis and ensure there is accountability to measure the success of the strategy. It is the responsibility of the Board of Directors to ensure there is an effective and active public relations committee.

Organizational Implications

In addition to further studies for services to the community, the study recommendations identified two broad categories that would enable the club to identify both the members' expectations and the community's needs. The categories are: (a) the need for a strategic plan to implement short range plans and long range plans to ensure continuity within the organization when leadership changes every one to two years, and (b) the Club Leadership Plan for the step-by-step process to implement the strategic plan. The strategic plan will ensure that all members are involved and have the opportunity to participate.

Strategic Planning

Strategic planning is to develop a clearly defined and understood plan about where the organization wishes to go and to keep continuity that exists from the prior year (Tretter & Tuttle, 2005, pp. 69–70). The best time for your leadership team to have a strategic planning session is at least two to four months prior to the beginning of their term of office (p. 70).

> Just doing the same things over and over again will not likely produce ongoing successful results. In any successful organization, that success can be traced back to a commitment of setting and following a specific plan of action intended to move the organization in a positive direction (p. 69).

The input of the members will identify what the member needs are and how to ensure that members are given the opportunity to meet these needs. In addition, the strategic planning session will identify the community services the club members wish to provide and the process with which to provide these services. It is imperative that this planning session is done properly and conducted as an efficient and effective process to obtain the relevant information to make good decisions. Therefore, it is my recommendation that the club obtain the services of a professional facilitator to lead this session and prepare a report that is useful and beneficial to the members.

The strategic plan will include the following issues identified by the members, the Hecate Strait Club, and the community: (a) what members want and need; (b) how to address the lack of knowledge of Rotary by the public; (c) the changes members would like within the organization; (d) how funds should be distributed into the community; (e) how the club can assist the City of Prince Rupert; and (f) how the two Rotary Clubs can work together.

In tandem with the strategic plan, it is recommended that the club implement the Rotary Leadership Plan (Rotary International, Leadership Education and Training Division, 2005), which provides the step-by-step process to implement the strategic plan of the members.

Club Leadership Plan

The strategic plan will identify the issues of the members, club, and the community. The Club Leadership Plan will aid in the implementation of the strategic plan. To address these recommendations, it is recommended that the District 5040 be asked to participate with the implementation plan and help members understand the Club Leadership Plan (Rotary International, Leadership Education and Training Division, 2005). It is further suggested that the District Governor of District 5040 be invited to explain the Club Leadership Plan to the members and give assistance with the implementation. The District Governor, who is the representative for the Rotary International President, is the most knowledgeable person to assist the club to embrace and implement the Club Leadership Plan.

"The club leadership plan is the recommended administrative structure for Rotary Clubs. It is based on the best practices of effective Rotary Clubs" (Rotary International, Leadership Education and Training Division, 2005, ¶ 1). The goal of the Club Leadership Plan is to create an effective club that pursues the Object of Rotary (Rotary International, 2007a, ¶ 1–5) and to carry out activities along each

"Avenue of Service" (Rotary International, Leadership Education and Training Division, 2005, ¶ 4).

> The Avenues of Service are classified as (1) Club Service focusing on strengthening fellowship and ensuring the effective functioning of the club, (2) vocational service encouraging Rotarians to serve others through their vocations and practicing high ethical standards, (3) community service covering the projects and activities the club undertakes to improve life in its community, and (4) International service encompassing actions taken to expand humanitarian reach around the globe and promoting world understanding and peace (¶ 4).

The issues identifying the members and community needs can be accomplished by the club conducting a strategic planning session with all the members as recommended by the Rotary Leadership Plan (Rotary International, Leadership Education and Training Division, 2005). This session will include all members given the opportunity to be involved and having input into the current and future affairs of the organization. It is very important that "everyone feel involved and is important. . . . One of the best ways to keep members involved is to make sure that they feel they're making a contribution to the group" (Jones et al., 2001, p. 259).

Evaluation

"Accountability is the rallying cry of today's organizations, and continuous measurement of individuals, teams, businesses, and institutions is considered to be the vehicle (Fenwick & Parsons, 2000, p. 13). The authors, discussing the purposes of evaluation, continued: "accountability asks three questions: Who is responsible? What are they responsible for? To whom are they responsible?" (p. 13). It is very important that the Rotary Club establish an evaluation process to measure the outcomes of activities of the club, of the committees, and the various projects and services. "Evaluation can be used to make decisions about changes to the program" (p. 15).

Implementation of Recommendations

"The power in organizations is the capacity generated by relationships" (Wheatley, 1999, p. 39) and people knowing how to listen and speak to each other. The literature review confirmed that our best knowledge already exists within our own organization. The strategy is to accomplish the organizational goals and how to apply this knowledge for maximum benefit.

Implementation of recommendations will produce trained quality leaders able to take the Rotary Club of Prince Rupert to the next level of excellence. Good leadership and good communications will produce leaders who will ensure members' needs are met, a healthy active organization, and a community that recognizes and acknowledges the good work of Rotary. The organization will meet the members' needs to give back to the community in both funds and services. The process of selecting recipients for funds will be seen as open and unbiased by the public. Funds given to needy or worthy organizations will offer endless opportunities for the Rotary Club to get known in the community. There will be opportunities for the Rotary Club to inform the public as to how Rotary raises it funds and the many projects and services the Rotary Club supports.

The participants stated, although the Rotary Club does good work, the public is not very aware of its value to the community. An effective and active public relations committee would oversee dissemination of information so the public can become aware of the work and value of Rotary. Knowledge of the Rotary Club was seen to be minimal in the community. Participants believe an organization well known for excellence in community service would be better able to entice members to join.

The community was less aware of the services the Rotary Club provided to international projects and issues of other countries. An active and purposeful Foundation Committee will enable members to make decisions as to international projects. This new mandate for the Foundation Committee will make the committee active and purposeful rather than just fund raising once a year.

Participants strongly expressed their desire for fellowship and friendships the Rotary Club offers. Members want the opportunity to enjoy the social aspects of the Rotary Club. Participants of the first focus group and the World Café expressed how noon meetings of the Rotary Club offered opportunity for fellowship and friendship. It is imperative the quality of these noon meetings offer the members what they need and want.

Membership matters will give the Rotary Club valuable information of the expectations of the new members. Information from members who leave the club is equally important, as this information can be used by the leaders of the club to act upon changes and actions required to address these issues. Information collected can be used to improve the Rotary Club to better meet the needs of the members. "Allowing volunteers to change tasks and roles, for example—in order not only to recognize but to take advantage of changing volunteers motivations" (Ilsley, 1990, p. 31). This will ensure members are committed because they are interested and challenged with new roles and responsibilities

Learning and training was identified by most participants as very important. Opportunities for members to enrol in the Rotary Leadership Institute (Rotary Leadership Institute, District 5040, 2007c, ¶ 1–7) will give members training in leadership. This will give the Rotary Club the potential for future good leaders. Participants stated personal growth is valued by all members and learning was frequently mentioned as important to the members.

"Forming partnerships within the faction one is working in, creating allies across the boundaries between factions, and finding confidants who are outside the field of action altogether is critical to the art of adaptive leadership" (Parks, 2005, p. 86). Partnerships with the Hecate Strait Rotary Club, City Hall, and service provider organizations will enhance the value of Rotary to the community. Organizations can work together to develop a needs assessment with regards to youth services. A Gap Analysis can be initiated by the Rotary Club to ensure that service organizations are not duplicating services to the community. It is not the intent that Rotary should do this study, but rather to be the catalyst that initiates the process.

Implications if Recommendations Are not Implemented

The implications of not making changes will lead to a lethargic membership, loss of members, ineffective committees, and lunch meetings that are attended by only those members who feel they must attend and not because they want to attend. It is imperative for the Rotary Club to be cognizant that "in reality, many organizations/ groups go into reverse or even crumble when the wrong leadership team takes over" (Tretter & Tuttle, 2005, p. 8).

Not making changes will deny members the opportunity to serve or to be involved in community service, and ultimately, members will leave the organization and seek other activities that will provide them with the challenges they seek. Members will not expand their knowledge of the world's needs and challenges.

The implications of not making changes will lead to loss of members who will not have the opportunity to enjoy fellowship and friendship. Participants identified that this was very important to the members. Lack of social aspects can lead to loss of members and also difficulty in attracting new members.

Long-time members will leave or take early retirement if they are not given roles of responsibilities and challenging activities. Some will leave if they believe that no one notices they have not been attending meetings. "Some organizations lose volunteer because they continually treat the volunteers as if they were new and had new volunteers' motives" (Ilsley, 1990, p. 31).

The implications of not making changes will see an organization that is stagnant. Members will be placed on committees in which they have no interest or an organization that does not know what the member wants. Soon, both long-time members and new members will leave unhappy that he or she was not doing what was expected. Ilsley (1990) confirmed, "volunteers choose an organization that seems likely to fulfill the desires expressed in their initial motivations They enter the organization full of expectations and enthusiasm and with very clear ideas of their reasons for joining" (p. 31).

The implications of not making changes will lead to membership that is not growing in personal knowledge of Rotary or challenged by new information. Such a membership does not grow or remain engaged.

"Not forming partnerships will lead to small groups of people trying to do activities that require more hands to do the projects" (Focus Group Participant #2). Cooperation and partnerships will not develop if groups and organizations do not meet to discuss mutual interests and activities. Equally important is the follow-up to ensure that decisions or objectives made are followed through and acted upon. If actions are not carried out, the credibility is gone, future relationships are lost.

Finally, the participants were concerned the good work of the Rotary Club is going unnoticed by the public. The possibility of members not being interested in doing community services because "no one neither notices nor appreciates it" can reduce the Rotary Club to a "fellowship club." Members who want to give back to the community, to who service the primary reason for being a member, would not be willing to remain in the Club. Loss of good members will result in the decline of the organization.

Therefore, as leaders of the Rotary Club, it is your duty to entice your members to be enrolled to achieve commitment and satisfaction, by identifying and seizing the opportunities to become a stronger volunteer organization. Conversely, the Rotary Club needs to be cognizant of what will happen to the organization, if the members do not address this opportunity for growth and change

Implications for Future Research

"Instead of responding to research findings as though they represent an absolute truth, use the findings as an opportunity to think about the social world around you" (Glesne, 2006, p. 213). This need for other research was very evident in my research study. The Rotary Club, and the enthusiasm of its members to do things and their "let me help" attitude can find itself venturing into projects before all the information is considered, and the outcomes of the projects can be jeopardized.

Therefore, a major benefit to the Rotary Club, the City of Prince Rupert, and volunteer organizations would be a Gap Analysis of the services that exist within the community and what needs are not provided. It is not the intent of this study to suggest that Rotary do this study, but Rotary could be the force that makes it happen.

Further study is also necessary regarding the youth issues in Prince Rupert. It is important to research what information already exists regarding the youth and their issues. There are many organizations already involved in the youth, and it would be beneficial to determine what organizations already exists and in what area Rotary can be effectively involved.

> Stringer (1999) suggested a social analysis to identify the groups that have a stake in the problem under consideration, so that men and women for all age, social class, ethnic, racial and religious groups, in all agencies, institutions, and organizations, feel that they have a voice in the proceedings (p. 50).

This study would be very valuable for any further research conducted in Prince Rupert.

The final research that would benefit service organizations is to study volunteerism in Prince Rupert and what motivates the volunteers into service. It would be valuable to inventory the volunteer organizations that exist and define their purpose and mandate. This will determine where there is a duplication of services and determine how each organization can contribute to the overall services of the community. A further inventory of volunteers that exist within the community would be valuable and inclusive, ensuring all interested volunteers are asked to participate.

Conclusion

My research question, "How can the Rotary Club of Prince Rupert best expand its volunteer service to the community?" is answered by this study. Through this action research project, I witnessed how the volunteers became committed as a result of their participation, their desire to serve became evident, and they became renewed in their commitment to serve. Rotary is "Service Above Self" (Rotary International, 2007d, ¶ 2) and a reminder to all Rotarians that it is about the other person.

> Don't ever let anyone convince you that you have no power—together we have the power to change the world. All significant changes in the world start slowly, at a single time and place, with a single action. One man, one woman, one child stands up and commits to creating a better world. Their courage inspires others, who begin to stand up themselves. You can be that person (Jones et al., 2001, p. 6).

CHAPTER SIX: LESSONS LEARNED

The following is a summation of the more significant lessons learned from the conduct of research. If I could start again with the knowledge I have gained since embarking on this path of learning, how much more effective and efficient I would be in conducting this research project and in writing my report. In this chapter, will share the successes and challenges that I faced during this entire process. I will start from the beginning with the ethical review approval, to the research process, and end with the challenges of the writing the thesis. I share Drucker's (1990) comment, "It is always painful to me to see how great the gap is between what I should have done and what I did do" (p. 224). It is hoped my lessons learned with help another learner to move closed to what should be done.

Leading up to the Research

Beginning with a plan is the most necessary first step for a major journey such as this. Nevertheless, even the most carefully thought-out prepared plans do go astray, but with a plan in place, unexpected crises are more manageable. It is the unexpected that causes the most difficulty, and generally it is because you "do not know what you do not know."

My major projected started very smoothly. My research question was a perfect match for me, and I was totally committed to my research project. It is very important that great care be taken when selecting the research question and sub-questions. The research question is the motivation that will take you to your ultimate goal. My research involved the Rotary Club, volunteer organizations, and the community. I was fortunate I had many years of volunteer service in a variety of organizations that gave me the knowledge and understanding of volunteer organizations.

My Faculty Advisor for LEAD563 supported my research project and gave me the confidence I could do this. He also advised me to finish chapter three of the Major Project Proposal (MPP) prior to attending residency two.

Prior to becoming a Master of Arts in Leadership and Training (MALT) learner, I knew very little about the *Publication Manual of the American Psychological Association* (2002), and its American Psychological Association (APA) approach to academic writing. I spent much time reading the manual and hoping I would eventually understand. I consistently practiced APA in all my writing. In hindsight, it would have been so valuable had I obtained the electronic version of APA. This would have saved me considerable time searching through the written text. "Search and find" is a much more efficient way to locate information. Unfortunately, I was not aware of an electronic version of APA until just recently.

To comply with APA standards (which is the writing style of the American Psyhological Association) , every book I read, I would reference the book in my journal with the author's full name, date, name of the book, date, publisher address, and name of the publisher. I was very specific when I wrote the references ensuring total accuracy at all times. As I proceeded with the Literature Review, I would write every quote that I thought might be of value or was of interest to me. Each quote would be written exactly as in the book and with the reference and page number. Research on the Internet was also documented with accuracy and completeness. This was very valuable, as I did not have to spend frustrating time looking for something I recalled reading somewhere.

During residency two, my confidence began to erode when I became aware my initial plans for a project supervisor came to an abrupt end. I was advised I could not have the project supervisor I had nominated. This created considerable panic and chaos in my plans, as I really wanted this project supervisor. He understood Rotary as he was a Rotarian. It was very important to have a supervisor who shared my interest in my project.

Perhaps this disappointment of losing my first supervisor and the frantic search for a new supervisor added to my confusion of the ethics review process and the timelines required. Although I attended the ethics review discussions during residency two, it was apparent I did not clearly understand. I had thought my Major Project Proposal was the basis for the ethics review. Had I realized the ethics review approval process was separate, I would have started this immediately after residency two. It was not until I was ready to start my research that I became aware there was a review process that had to be approved.

Finally, I became aware there was more to the ethics review than I had anticipated. It was my fellow cohort learners who showed me the way. Being in constant contact with some of my fellow learners was the most valuable source of help throughout this entire programme. Without my cohort, my journey could have been chaotic.

Now armed with new knowledge of the ethics review process, I completed the ethics review application without too much delay. I received approval very quickly. I acknowledge this ease of approval was also due to the intense monitoring and guidance from my new supervisor.

Back to planning, I had developed a project timeline that was reasonable and achievable and I monitored it regularly. Whenever I realized that I was not on schedule, I would immediately amend it so it was achievable. However, I was cognizant not to give myself permission to change my timelines without good reason. Always, I had the completion date in mind, and that date could not be adjusted; but, in the end, I did have to adjust the finish date as it was just not possible to obtain the chapter approvals as quickly as I anticipated. I regret that I was still trying to finish within two weeks of the deadline. This did not suit my way of doing things. I know if I was to do this again I would ensure I met my target finish time. Doing things under pressure is just not a good way. I was fortunate that I had the flexibility in my work to take time from my work to devote to writing my thesis. Without this time totally dedicated to writing, I might not have finished in time to graduate in June.

A valuable resource was the ethics department and the thesis department. Their response to my emails were almost immediate and always with a suggested recommendation or interpretation of the rules. They were a wealth of knowledge and extremely willing to assist and give advice. Another valuable resource was the library, and they would help me find reference books I required.

I recognized early in my research there were some special requirements for my project and submitted requests for permissions for use of copywritten and other organizational documents well in advance and received them very promptly. I would strongly recommend that the learner review at the beginning of his or her research which documents and copyrights might be required and pursue permissions immediately.

Another misunderstanding I had was in preparation for residency two, when I read we were not to start any research before residency. I interpreted that to mean that I was not to read about research or to familiarize myself with research. I thought this was to ensure that I did not have any preconceived ideas of how to conduct research. This was not the case. What was meant was "no actual physical research" was to commence before residency two.

In retrospect, it would have been so valuable to have read books such as *The Craft of Research* (2nd ed.) by Booth et al. (2003), or *Practical Research: Planning and Design* (8th ed.) by Leedy and Ormrod (2005). I would have been so much better prepared for residency two.

The Research

Data Collection

Once I completed residency two, I delved into research books on how to conduct research. I read copious books on focus groups, World Café, interviews, and surveys. I made notes in my journal from all of these books documenting accurate references and page numbers. Once

I received my ethics review approval, I was ready to commence data collections.

I personalized all my communications and invitations to participants in my research. Every correspondence and email was labelled and filed onto my computer with relevant file folders. Naming and organizing the file folders are very important. A good filing system will add to ease of locating information. Also, I converted all my emails into portable document format (PDF) documents and filed them in the relevant folders.

All the versions of each chapter were filed in the appropriate chapters; but as I kept revising my chapters, the files would become confusing, and then as the chapters were returned by my supervisor or the editor. It added to the confusion as to which document I should be working on or had been working on. I eventually named the file folders according to chapters and then used the current date for naming the sub-folders. I ensured the current chapter I was working on would go into the current date. Therefore, I always knew which file was the one I used last. This became very important, as towards the end of the project I found myself working on three chapters at one time. I was given the advice by my project supervisor to work on one chapter at a time. Working on one chapter at a time worked well for the early chapters, but my thought process needed to connect each chapter with the other. Working on one chapter at a time did not work for me.

Testing Focus Group Questions

I developed my research questions during residency two and many of the cohorts helped me write the questions appropriate to my research. I had asked for feedback on my questions during the Major Project Display event. I subsequently tested these questions on Rotarians and non-Rotarians when I returned home. Therefore, by the time I was ready to commence my research; my questions were ready and tested. I recommend this process, as it eliminated stress and panic at the last moments. As the final steps, I sent my research questions to my supervisor and sponsor for comment and feedback

Planning Events

I had anticipated difficulty in obtaining consent forms as Rotarians are not familiar with this type of rigour. However, there was no problem in obtaining consent forms from Rotarians. I did have one Rotarian refuse to sign a consent form. I commented that anyone who did not sign consent was welcome to remain, but I could not use his/her information since I did not have the consent to do so. I then carried on with the meeting.

Keeping track of all the things that need to be done can be a daunting task for people who are not familiar with organizing events or time management. As I had considerable experience in planning events, I was well organized. I used a journal to write down all the things that need to be done, and I would check them off as completed. I would check the journal daily to ensure I had not missed anything. I would recommend this procedure to anyone organizing events or activities.

The Events

The Rotary Club members' focus group was excellent, and I served food and soft drinks to set the social atmosphere. I would not do anything differently, and I was extremely pleased with the event. The participants expressed enjoyment of the meeting and participated with enthusiasm. The Hecate Strait Rotary Club's focus group was held during their lunch meeting and conducted as an open forum to encourage the participants to make comments.

The World Café was fun, and the members' enjoyment of the lunchtime event was enlightening. I discussed the duties with each facilitator and recorder prior to the meeting. In retrospect, I should have emailed a sheet of instructions as to their responsibilities and my expectations. However, each facilitator and recorder did an excellent job collecting valuable and appropriate information.

Food is very important and should be appropriate for the event. I had met with the chef of the hotel and discussed the lunch menu. The Rotary members enjoyed the change of menu. The World Café was scheduled from noon to 1:15 p.m., which is the regular Rotary noon meeting time. I was fortunate that the President allowed me the entire meeting for the World Café, and no Rotary business was conducted. One hour and fifteen minutes was not sufficient time, but I needed to consider the members' need to return to work. The World Café began on time and ended on time.

The one-on-one interviews were an excellent method for obtaining information. The participants were eager to discuss the questions and many times would offer their personal insights and experiences to explain their answers. The allotted time of half an hour was ample time to obtain all the information I required from each participant.

Surveys were my least effective method of information gathering. I would have gained so much more insight had I held interviews with the service provider organizations. Although their answers to my survey questions were excellent and very useful, I feel that I could have gained more useful information had I interviewed the participants.

The lack of response to the surveys from the public was disappointing. This non response indicated to me that the people were not interested or felt their input had no value. Had I conducted an interview, I would have conveyed to each citizen how important their input was to my research. Another reason for lack of survey participation may have been the invitation to participate in my research stated that they may decline to participate. This could mean permission not to respond. Since I had stated that there was no requirement to participate and their refusal would have not implications, I did not wish to do follow-up requests for fear it could be interpreted as being coercive. Therefore, I did not do any follow-ups to my invitation to the citizens to participate.

Rogelberg and Stanton (2007), commenting on non-response bias, stated the researcher's major efforts and resources should go into understanding the magnitude and direction of bias caused by non-response (¶ 9). The survey of the public was not a major part of the research, as the data collection of the information of the public was well represented by the City Councillors, administration staff, and service provider organizations.

Data Analysis

After I completed the data gathering, I was cognizant of the importance of data analysis. This was the most difficult part of the study. Booth et al. (2003) stated, "Determine what kind of evidence that your readers will expect in support of your answer" (p. 38). Therefore, I took great care in the data analysis, as this process has the greatest influence on the success of the research.

As stated by Leedy and Ormrod (2005), "The human mind is undoubtedly the most important tool on the researcher's workbench.

Its functioning dwarfs all other gadgetry. Nothing equals its powers of comprehension, integrative reasoning, and insight" (p. 31). I was cognizant that the data analysis may be influenced by my thought process and interpretations, yet, being cognizant that nothing can replace the human mind.

Triangulation

Triangulation was very important to my research, as validity and trust worthiness were criterion I had established. I used all four methods of focus groups, interviews, World Café, and surveys. Glesne (1999) stated that "the credibility of your findings and interpretations depends upon your careful attention to establishing trustworthiness" (p. 151). Merriam (1988) stated, "Triangulation strengthens reliability as well as internal validity" (p. 207).

Writing the Major Project

The best procedure I had was to keep journals of all the information and quotes I found interesting. I kept these organized so they would be easy to find. I liked the hand written recording of the journal, and by the end of my major project, I had five journals. Not all were filled, but each contained massive amounts of information.

Booth et al. (2003) described the same procedures that I used. Although I had not read this previously, this was the most valuable procedure and helped in writing and finding the resources without hunting and looking. They stated, "Before you start taking notes, record all bibliographical data. We promise that no habit will serve you better for the rest of your career, author, title, editions, volume, place published, publisher, date, published page number of article or chapters editors, if any (p. 97).

For online sources, record as much of the above information as applies: uniform resource locator, date of access, and webmaster (if any). Ensure to take full notes. When you are hunting down data, it can feel tedious to record them all accurately, but you can lose what you gain from reading carefully if your notes do not reflect the quality of your thinking. Some still believe that the best notes are written longhand (p. 98).

"Writing is a lonely process. While writing about people and social processes, you paradoxically remove yourself from the world of human beings" (Glesne, 1999, p. 160). I liked writing alone. I wrote what came into my head. Once that was done, I planned the chapter and rearrange the content. The hardest part of writing is getting started. Therefore, it is important to begin writing.

Journey's End

I recorded the lessons learned in my journal as soon as I became aware of them so that I would not forget them. It is hoped that my comments will help future researchers to learn what I found useful and helpful, and my challenges will help avoid some of the pitfalls for anyone venturing on the research path. I am amazed at how much I have learned, and if I could do it all over again, the road would be less difficult.

It is my endeavour that in some way I have made a difference. If so, then I have achieved success.

> The world changes every day because of research, not always for the better. But done well, research is crucial to improving every facet of our lives. It is no exaggeration to say that your research and your reports of it can improve perhaps not the whole world, but at least your corner of it (Booth et al., 2003, p 12).

REFERENCES

American Psychological Association. (2002). *Publication manual of the American Psychological Association* (5th ed.). Washington, DC: Author.

Bacharach, S. B. (2005). *Get them on your side.* Avon, MA: Platinum Press.

BC Stats. (2007). *British Columbia municipal census populations 1921 to 2006: City of Prince Rupert.* Retrieved September 10, 2007, from http://www.bcstats.gov.bc.ca/data/pop/pop/mun/mun1921_2006.asp

Beck, U. (2005). *The brave new world of work.* Cambridge: Polity Press

Beem, C. (1999). *The necessity of politics: Reclaiming American public life.* Chicago: University of Chicago Press.

Bellman, G. M. (1990). *The consultant's calling: Bringing who you are to what you do.* San Francisco: Jossey-Bass.

Bellman, G. M. (2002). *The consultant's calling: Bringing who you are to what you do* (2nd ed.). San Francisco: Jossey-Bass.

Bennis, W. G., & Goldsmith, J. (2003). *Learning to lead: A workbook on becoming a leader* (3rd ed.). New York: Basic Books.

Booth, W. C., Colomb, G. G., & Williams, J. M. (2003). *The craft of research* (2nd ed.). Chicago: University of Chicago Press.

Brown, J., & Isaacs, D. (2005). *World Café: Shaping our futures through conversations that matter.* San Francisco: Berrett-Koehler.

Bussell, H., & Forbes, D. (2001). Understanding the volunteer market: The what, where, who and why of volunteering. *International Journal of Nonprofit and Sector Marketing, 7*(3), 244.

Butcher, J. (2003). *A humanistic perspective on the volunteer-recipient relationship.* In P. Dekker and L. Halman (eds.). *The values of volunteering: Cross-cultural perspectives* (pp 111-125), New York: Plenum.

Canadian Institutes of Health Research, Natural Sciences and Engineering Research Council of Canada, Social Sciences and Humanities Research Council of Canada. (1998). *Tri-council policy statement: Ethical conduct for research involving humans* (with 2000, 2002 and 2005 amendments). Retrieved April 10, 2006, from http://www.pre.ethics.gc.ca/english/policystatement/policystatement.cfm

Carver, C. (2002). *On board leadership.* San Francisco: Jossey-Bass.

City of Prince Rupert. (2007). *Official community plan of the City of Prince Rupert.* Retrieved February 18, 2008, from http://www.princerupert.ca/page.php

Clary, E. G., & Snyder, M. (1999). The motivations to volunteer: Theoretical and practical considerations. *Current Directions in Psychological Science, 8*(5), 156

Creswell, J. W. (2003). *Research design: Qualitative, quantitative, and mixed methods approaches* (2nd ed.). Thousand Oaks, CA: Sage.

Dekker, P., & Halman, L. (Eds.). (2003). *The values of volunteering: Cross-cultural perspectives.* New York: Kluwer Academic/PlenumPublishers.

Denzin, N. K. (1989). *Interpretive interactions.* Newbury Park, CA: Sage.
DePree, M. (2003). *Leading without power: Finding hope in serving community.* San Francisco: Jossey-Bass.

Devlyn, F. (2001). *Frank talk: How you can make a difference in your career, your community, and your world through membership in Rotary.* Evanston, IL: Rotary International.

Dingle, A. (2000). *Measuring volunteering: A practical toolkit.* Retrieved January 22, 2007, from http://www.IndependentSector.org

Drucker, P. F. (1990). *Managing the nonprofit organization: Principles and practices.* New York: Harpercollins.

Durkin, D. (2007). *Engaging four generations to enhance productivity.* Retrieved May 15, 2007, from http://www.clomedia.com/includes/printcontent.php?aid=1709

Eli, F. (2006). *Major project documents on rotary awareness in Prince Rupert.* Prince Rupert, BC, Canada: Author.

Eliasoph, N. (2003). *Cultivating apathy in voluntary associations.* In P. Dekker and L. Halman (eds.). *The values of volunteering: Cross-cultural perspectives* (pp. 199-212). New York: Plenum.

Fenwick, Y., & Parsons, J. (2000). *The art of evaluation: A handbook for educators and trainers.* Toronto, ON, Canada: Thompson Educational Publishing.

Fredricksson, L-O. (2007). *A new look at global ethics and the four-way test.* Retrieved November 1, 2007, from http://www.rotary.org/en/MediaAndNews/News/Pages/070917_news_Four-WayTest.aspx

Fullan, M. (2001). *Leading in a culture of change.* San Francisco: Jossey-Bass.

Gann, N. (1996). *Managing change in voluntary organizations: A guide to practice.* Bristol, PA: Open University Press.

Glesne, C. (2006). *Becoming qualitative researchers: An introduction* (3rd ed.). New York: Pearson

Halman, L. (2003). *Volunteering, democracy, and democratic attitudes.* In P. Dekker & L. Halman (Eds.), *The values of volunteering: Cross-cultural perspectives* (pp. 179-198). New York: Plenum.

Hamlin, S. (2006). *How to talk so people listen: Connecting in today's workplace.* New York: HarperCollins.

Hodgkinson, V. A. (2003). *Volunteering in global perspective.* In P. Dekker & L. Halman (Eds.), *The values of volunteering: Cross-cultural perspectives* (pp. 35-53), New York: Plenum.

Hybels, B. (2004). *The volunteer revolution: Unleashing the power of everybody.* Grand Rapids, MI: Zondervan.

Ilsley, P. J. (1990). *Enhancing the volunteer experience.* San Francisco, CA: Jossey-Bass.

Inglehart, R. (2003). *Modernization and volunteering.* In P. Dekker & L. Halman (Eds.), *The values of volunteering: Cross-cultural perspectives* (pp. 55-70). New York: Plenum.

Jones, E., Haenfler, R., & Johnson, B. (with Klocke, B.). (2001). *The better world handbook: from good intentions to everyday actions.* Gabriola Islands, BC, Canada: New society Publishers.

Knowles, M. S., Holton, E. F., III, & Swanson, R. A. (2005). *The adult learner: The definitive classic in adult education and human resource development.* San Diego, CA: Elsevier.

Kouzes, J. M., & Posner, B. Z. (2002). *The leadership challenge: The most rusted source on becoming a better leader* (3rd ed.). San Francisco: Jossey-Bass.

Krueger, R. A., & Casey, M. A. (2000). *Focus groups: A practical guide for applied research* (3rd ed.). Thousand Oaks, CA: Sage.
Krueger, R. A. (1998). *Analyzing and reporting focus group results: Focus group kit 6.* Thousand Oaks, CA: Sage.

Krueger, R. A. (1998). *Developing questions for focus groups: Focus group kit 3.* Thousand Oaks, CA: Sage.

Ladd, E. C. (1999). *The Ladd report: Startling new research shows how an explosion of voluntary groups, activities, and charitable donations is transforming our towns and cities.* New York: Simon & Schuster.

Leblanc, R., & Gillies, J. (2005). *Inside the boardroom: How boards really work and the coming revolution in corporate governance.* Mississauga, ON, Canada: John Wiley & Sons.

Leedy, P. D., & Ormrod, J. E. (2005). *Practical research: Planning and design* (8th ed.). Upper Saddle River, NJ: Pearson Prentice Hall.

MacKeracher, D. (2006). *Making sense of adult learning* (2nd ed.). Toronto, ON, Canada: University of Toronto Press.

MacLeod, F., & Hogarth, S. (1999). *Leading today's volunteers: Motivate and mange your team.* Vancouver, BC, Canada: Self-Counsel Press.

Merriam, S. B. (1998). *Qualitative research and case study applications in education.* San Francisco: Jossey-Bass.

Morgan, D. L. (1997). *Focus groups as qualitative research* (2nd ed.). Thousand Oaks, CA: Sage.

Palmer, P. J. (1998). *The courage to teach: Exploring the inner landscape of a teacher's life.* San Francisco: Jossey-Bass.

Palys, T. (2003). *Research decisions: Quantitative and qualitative perspectives* (3rd ed.). Scarborough, ON, Canada: Nelson.

Parks, S. D. (2005). *Leadership can be taught: A bold approach for a complex world.* Boston: Harvard Business School Press.

Putnam, R. D. (2000). *Bowling alone: The collapse and revival of American community.* New York: Simon & Schuster.

Quinn, R. E. (2004). *Building the bridge as you walk on it: A guide for leading change.* San Francisco: Jossey-Bass.

Riggio, R. E., & Orr, S. S. (2004). *Improving leadership in non profit organizations.* San Francisco: John Wiley & Sons.

Rogelberg, S. G., & Stanton, J. M. (2007). Introduction: Understanding and dealing with organizational survey nonresponse. *Organizational Research Methods, 10,* 195-209. Retrieved February 19, 2008, from Sage Publications Online database.

Rotary Club of Prince Rupert. (2006). *Constitution and by-laws.* Prince Rupert, BC, Canada: Author.

Rotary International. (2007a). *Guiding principles.* Retrieved October 21, 2007, from http://www.rotary.org/en/AboutUs/RotaryInternational/GuidingPrinciples/Pages/ridefault.aspx

Rotary International. (2007b). *Manual of procedures: A reference manual for Rotary leaders.* Evanston, IL.

Rotary International. (2007c). *Programs of Rotary International.* Retrieved November 1, 2007 from http://www.rotary.org/en/AboutUs/RotaryInternational/Programs/Pages/ridefault.aspx

Rotary International. (2007d). *Rotary International.* Retrieved November 1, 2007, from http://www.rotary.org/en/AboutUs/RotaryInternational/Pages/ridefault.aspx

Rotary International. (2007e). *Rotary International History.* Retrieved November 1, 2007, from http://www.rotary.org/en/AboutUs/RotaryInternational/History/Pages/ridefault.aspx

Rotary International. (2007f). *Service and fellowship.* Retrieved November 1, 2007, from http://www.rotary.org/en/ServiceAndFellowship/Pages/ridefault.aspx

Rotary International. (2007g). *Structure: Overview of Rotary International's leadership structure.* Retrieved November 22, 2007, from http://www.rotary.org/en/AboutUs/RotaryLeadership/Structure/Pages/ridefault.aspx

Rotary International. (2007h). *Students and youth.* Retrieved November 1, 2007 from http://www.rotary.org/EN/STUDENTSANDYOUTH/Pages/ridefault.aspx

Rotary International District 5040. (2007a). *District assembly.* Retrieved March 12, 2008, from http://www.clubrunner.ca/dprg/dxhome/dxeventstab/_eventitem.aspx?did=5040&index=3280&linkcat=5&dir=f&tail=1

Rotary International District 5040. (2007b). *District manual 2007-2008: Rotary shares.* (Available from District 5040, Directory Chair, Unit 250 8833 Otlin Crescent, Richmond, BC, Canada, V6X 3Z7)

Rotary International District 5040. (2007c). *Rotary Leadership Institute.* Retrieved February 2, 2008, from http://www.clubrunner.ca/dprg/dxprogramhome/_programhome.aspx?did=5040&pageid=20974

Rotary International, Leadership Education and Training Division. (2005). *Club leadership plan.* Retrieved October 15, 2007, from http://www.rotary.org/RIdocuments/en_pdf/245en.pdf

Royal Roads University. (2007). *Research ethics policy.* Retrieved April 5, 2007, from http://www.royalroads.ca/research/ethical-reviews/ethics-policy.htm

Secretan, L. (1997). *Reclaiming higher ground: Creating organizations that inspire the soul.* Toronto, ON, Canada: MacMillan Canada.

Senge, P. (2006). *The fifth discipline: The art and practice of the learning organization* (rev. ed.). New York: Doubleday.

Statistics Canada. (2001). *Caring Canadians, involved Canadians: Highlights from the 2000 national survey of giving, volunteering and participating.* Retrieved February 19, 2007, from http://www.givingandvolunteering.ca/reports/2000_NSGVP_highlights.asp

Statistics Canada. (2005). *Caring Canadians, involved Canadians: Highlights from the 2004 national survey of giving, volunteering and participating.* Retrieved February 28, 2007, from http://www.givingandvolunteering.ca/pdf/CSGVP_Highlights_2004_en.pdf

Stebbins, R, A., & Graham, M. (Eds.). (2004). *Volunteering as leisure, leisure as volunteering: An international assessment.* Cambridge, MA: CABI Publishing.

Stringer, E. T. (1999). *Action research* (2nd ed.). Thousand Oaks, CA: Sage.

Thomas, T. H. (1974). *It's all in a lifetime: Way up north.* Auckland, New Zealand: Rotary Clubs of New Zealand.

Tretter, R. C., & Tuttle, B. R., Jr. (2005). *Leadership in volunteer groups: The essential guide for leadership and organization with any volunteer group.* Denton, NC: TnT.

Voicu, M., & Voicu, B. (2003). *Volunteering in Romania: A rara avis.* In P. Dekker & L. Halman (Eds.), *The values of volunteering: Cross-cultural perspectives* (pp. 143-159). New York: Plenum.

Wheatley, M. (1999). *Leadership and the new science: Discovering order in a chaotic world.* San Francisco: Barrett-Koehler.

Wolf, T. (1999). *Managing a nonprofit organization in the twenty-first century.* New York: Simon & Schuster.

Wolcott, H. F. (2001). *Writing up qualitative research* (2nd ed.). Thousand Oaks, CA: Sage.

Yukl, G. (2006). *Leadership in organizations* (6th ed.). Upper Saddle River, NJ: Pearson Prentice Hall

APPENDIX A: Consent Form for Participation in Focus Group #1

October 15, 2007

Dear

I hope that you will be able to attend the focus group on Wednesday, October 24, 2007, at 7:30 p.m. @ xxx xxxxx xxxxx Board Room. This project is part of the requirement for my Master's Degree in Leadership and Training at Royal Roads University. My credentials with Royal Roads University can be established by calling Dr. Gerry Nixon, Acting Director, School of Leadership Studies, at xxx xxx xxxx or emailing xxxx@xxxx.xx.

My interest in this research project is the result of my years with the Rotary Club of Prince Rupert. I have served as a director for four years and then as Secretary for almost five years. I became President and served from 2004 to 2005, served as Past President, and then served as Treasurer from 2006 to 2007.

This document constitutes an agreement to participate in my research project, the objective of which is to receive input to my research question: "How can the Rotary Club of Prince Rupert best expand its volunteer services to the community?" The sponsoring organization is the Rotary Club of Prince Rupert. All members of the Board of Directors are invited to participate.

The research will consist of a Focus Group and is expected to last one and a half (1.5) hours during an evening. The foreseen questions will refer to the volunteer services provided to the community by the Rotary Club of Prince Rupert and what you can suggest to best expand these services. In addition to submitting my final report to Royal Roads University in partial fulfillment for a Master's Degree in Leadership and Training, I will also be sharing my research findings with the members of the Rotary Club of Prince Rupert. The information (data) collected will be used in the preparation of my Major Project.

The facilitator for the Focus Group will be Ms. Jennifer Wilson, MA, who is a family member and has been contracted by the City of Prince Rupert to do various services for them. I have chosen Jennifer as she has the vast experience to ensure the success of this focus group. I have chosen a professional facilitator to ensure free and candid opinions from the participants.

Information will be recorded in handwritten or typed on word processor format and, where appropriate, summarized, in anonymous format, in the body of the final report. The focus group discussions will be audio recorded for accuracy. However, at no time will any specific comments be attributed to any individual unless specific agreement has been obtained beforehand.

- Please be advised that discussions within the focus group is to be respected as confidential information but participants will be advised to be cognizant that information in these public forums may cause loss of anonymity. However, the recording of the data and the reports will not identify the participants' comments.

- All documentation will be kept strictly confidential and destroyed at the completion of my Major Project. All raw data and transcripts will be retained for at least one year after publication of the Major Project and no more that five years, after which the data will be destroyed.

A copy of the final report will be available online from Royal Roads University and through UMI/Proquest and the Theses Canada portal. It will be publicly accessible and access and distribution will be unrestricted.

You are not compelled to participate in this research project. If you do choose to participate, you are free to withdraw at any time without prejudice. Similarly, if you choose not to participate in this research project, this information will also be maintained in confidence.

By signing this letter, you give free and informed consent to participate in this project.

Name: (Please Print): _____

Signed:_____

Date: _____

APPENDIX B: Consent Form for Participation in World Cafe

October 20, 2007

Dear

I am looking forward to your attendance at the World Café on Thursday, November 1, 2007, at the regular noon Rotary Meeting. This project is part of the requirement for my Master's Degree in Leadership and Training, at Royal Roads University. My credentials with Royal Roads University can be established by calling Dr. Gerry Nixon, Acting Director, School of Leadership Studies, at xxx xxx xxxx or emailing xxxx@xxxxxxx.xx.

This document constitutes an agreement to participate in my research project, the objective of which to receive input to my research question: "How can the Rotary Club of Prince Rupert better expand its volunteer services to the community?" The sponsoring organization is the Rotary Club of Prince Rupert.

The research will consist of World Cafe and is foreseen to last one (1.0) hours during Thursday noon meeting beginning at 12:15 pm sharp. The questions will refer to the volunteer services provided to the community by the Rotary Club of Prince Rupert and what you can suggest to best expand these services. In addition to submitting my final report to Royal Roads University in partial fulfillment for a Master's Degree in Leadership, I will also be sharing my research findings with the Rotary Club of Prince Rupert. The information (data) collected will be used in the preparation of my Major Project.

Information will be provided by you and it will be summarized, in anonymous format, in the body of the final report. At no time will any specific comments be attributed to any individual unless specific agreement has been obtained beforehand. All documentation will be kept strictly confidential.

A copy of the final report will be available online from Royal Roads University and through UMI/Proquest and the Theses Canada portal. It will be publicly accessible and access and distribution will be unrestricted.

You are not compelled to participate in this research project. If you do choose to participate, you are free to withdraw at any time without prejudice. Similarly, if you choose not to participate in this research project, this information will also be maintained in confidence.

By signing this letter, you give free and informed consent to participate in this project.

Name: (Please Print): _____

Signed: _____

Date: _____

APPENDIX C: Consent Form for Participation in an Interview

October 15, 2007

Councillor

Thank you for agreeing to meet with me for an Interview regarding my research project. This project is part of the requirement for my Master of Arts Degree in Leadership and Training, at Royal Roads University. My credentials with Royal Roads University can be established by calling Dr. Gerry Nixon, Acting Director, School of Leadership Studies, at xxx xxx xxxx or emailing xxxx@xxxxxxx.xx.

This document constitutes an agreement to participate in my research project, the objective of which to receive input to my research question: "How can the Rotary Club of Prince Rupert best expand its volunteer services to the community?" The sponsoring organization is the Rotary Club of Prince Rupert.

The research will consist of the interview and is foreseen to last one half (1/2) hour during a time that is mutually convenient. The questions will refer to the volunteer services provided to the community by the Rotary Club of Prince Rupert and what you can suggest to best expand these services.

In addition to submitting my final report to Royal Roads University in partial fulfillment for a Master of Arts degree in Leadership and Training, I will also be sharing my research findings with the Rotary Club of Prince Rupert. The information (data) collected will be used in the preparation of my Major Project.

Information will be recorded in hand-written format and, where appropriate, summarized, in anonymous format, in the body of the final report. At no time will any specific comments be attributed to any individual unless specific agreement has been obtained beforehand. All documentation will be kept strictly confidential.

A copy of the final report will be available online from Royal Roads University and through UMI/Proquest and the Theses Canada portal. It will be publicly accessible and access and distribution will be unrestricted.

You are not compelled to participate in this research project. If you do choose to participate, you are free to withdraw at any time without prejudice. Similarly, if you choose not to participate in this research project, this information will also be maintained in confidence.

Yours truly,

Nancy Eidsvik

By signing this letter, you give free and informed consent to participate in this project.

Name: (Please Print):_____ Date: _____

Signed: _____

APPENDIX D: Consent Form for Focus Group #2

November 9, 1007

Dear Members of the Hecate Strait Rotary Club:

This project is part of the requirement for my Master's Degree in Leadership and Training, at Royal Roads University. My credentials with Royal Roads University can be established by calling Dr. Gerry Nixon, Acting Director, School of Leadership Studies, at xxx xxx xxxx or emailing xxxx@xxxxxxx.xx.

My interest in this research project is the result of my years with the Rotary Club of Prince Rupert. I have served as a director for four years and then as Secretary for almost five years. I became President and served from 2004 to 2005, served as Past President, and then served as Treasurer from 2006 to 2007.

This document constitutes an agreement to participate in my research project, the objective of which to receive input to my research question: "How can the Rotary Club of Prince Rupert best expand its volunteer services to the community?" The sponsoring organization is the Rotary Club of Prince Rupert.

The research will consist of a Focus Group and is expected to last one half (.5) hour during your noon meeting. The foreseen questions will refer to the volunteer services provided to the community by the Rotary Club of Prince Rupert and what you can suggest to best expand these services and if the two clubs should work together for the benefit the community.

In addition to submitting my final report to Royal Roads University in partial fulfillment for a Master's Degree in Leadership and Training, I will also be sharing my research findings with the members of the Rotary Club of Prince Rupert. The information (data) collected will be used in the preparation of my Major Project.

Information will be recorded in handwritten or typed on word processor format and, where appropriate, summarized, in anonymous format, in the body of the final report. The focus group discussions will be audio recorded for accuracy. However, at no time will any specific comments be attributed to any individual unless specific agreement has been obtained beforehand.

- Please be advised that discussions within the focus group is to be respected as confidential information but participants will be advised to be cognizant that information in these public forums may cause loss of anonymity. However, the recording of the data and the reports will not identify the participants' comments.

- All documentation will be kept strictly confidential and destroyed at the completion of my Major Project. All raw data and transcripts will be retained for at least one year after publication of the Major Project and no more that five years, after which the data will be destroyed.

A copy of the final report will be available online from Royal Roads University and through UMI/Proquest and the Theses Canada portal. It will be publicly accessible and access and distribution will be unrestricted.

You are not compelled to participate in this research project. If you do choose to participate, you are free to withdraw at any time without prejudice. Similarly, if you choose not to participate in this research project, this information will also be maintained in confidence.

Yours truly,

Nancy Eidsvik

Nancy Eidsvik, MA

By signing this letter, you give free and informed consent to participate in this project.

Name: (Please Print): _____

Signed: _____

Date: _____

APPENDIX E: Consent Form for Survey

November 14, 2007

Dear

I am hoping that one of you would be able to participate in my research project that I am conducting. This project is part of the requirement for my Master of Arts degree in Leadership and Training, at Royal Roads University. My credentials with Royal Roads University can be established by calling Dr. Gerry Nixon, Acting Director, School of Leadership Studies, at xxx xxx xxxx or emailing xxxx@xxxxxxx.xx.

The objective of my research project is to obtain your input as to how you view the volunteer services provided to the community by the Rotary Club of Prince Rupert and what you can suggest to best expand these services. The sponsoring organization for this project is the Rotary Club of Prince Rupert. In addition I will be submitting my final report to Royal Roads University in partial fulfillment for a Master of Arts degree in Leadership and Training. I will also be sharing my research findings with the Rotary Club of Prince Rupert. The information (data) will be used for my Major Project Thesis.

A copy of the final report will be available online from royal Roads University, and through UMI/Proquest and the Theses Canada portal. It will be publicly accessible and access and distribution will be unrestricted.

You are not compelled to participate in this research project. If you do choose to participate, you are free to withdraw at any time without prejudice. Similarly, if you choose not to participate in this research project, this information will also be maintained in confidence. Approximately twenty organizations within Prince Rupert have been invited to participate and all those who accept will be sent the survey questions by their choice of email or mail

The completion and return or submission of this survey gives me the permission I require to use the information to prepare my research project. At no time will any specific comments be attributed to any individual. Anonymous quotations may be used in the final report in addition to the summarized information. All documentation will be kept strictly confidential and will be destroyed to ensure confidentially.

You may place your comments directly on this survey and mail it back to me to ensure it will be kept confidential upon receipt. I would appreciate the return before November 19, 2007.

Name: Nancy Eidsvik

Email: xxxx@xxxxxxx.xx

Telephone: (xxx) xxx xxxx

Thank you very much,

Nancy Eidsvik

APPENDIX F: Letter of Invitation to Focus Groups

Nancy Eidsvik

xxxxx xxxxx, xxxxxxxx, x.x., xxx xxx

October 1, 2007

To the Directors of the Rotary Club of

Dear

I would like to invite you to be part of a research project that I am conducting. This project is part of the requirement for a Master's Degree in Leadership and Training, at Royal Roads University. My credentials with Royal Roads University can be established by calling Dr. Gerry Nixon, Acting Director, School of Leadership Studies, at xx xxx xxxx or emailing xxxxx.xxxxx@xxxxx.xx. My interest in this research project is the result of my years with the Rotary Club of Prince Rupert. I have served as a director for four years and then as Secretary for almost five years. I became President and served from 2004 to 2005, served as past President, and then served as Treasurer from 2006 to 2007.

This document constitutes an agreement to participate in my research project, the objective of which to receive input to my research question: "How can the Rotary Club of Prince Rupert best expand its volunteer services to the community?" The sponsoring organization is the Rotary Club of Prince Rupert. All members of the Board of Directors are invited to participate.

The research will consist of a Focus Group and is expected to last one and a half (1.5) hours during an evening. The foreseen questions will refer to the volunteer services provided to the community by the Rotary Club of Prince Rupert and what you can suggest to best expand these services. In addition to submitting my final report to Royal Roads University in partial fulfillment for a Master's Degree in Leadership and Training, I will also be sharing my research findings with the members of the Rotary Club of Prince Rupert. The information (data) collected will be used in the preparation of my Major Project.

The facilitator for the Focus Group will be Ms. Jennifer Wilson, MA, who is a family member and has been contracted by the City of Prince Rupert to do various services for them. I have chosen Jennifer as she has the vast experience to ensure the success of this focus group. I have chosen a professional facilitator to ensure free and candid opinions from the participants.

Information will be recorded by hand or typed in word processor format and, where appropriate, summarized, in anonymous format, in the body of the final report. The focus group discussions will be audio recorded for accuracy. However, at no time will any specific comments be attributed to any individual unless specific agreement has been obtained beforehand.

- Please be advised that discussions within the focus group is to be respected as confidential information but participants will be advised to be cognizant that information in these public forums may cause loss of anonymity. However, the recording of the data and the reports will not identify the participants' comments.

- All documentation will be kept strictly confidential and destroyed at the completion of my Major Project. All raw data and transcripts will be retained for at least one year after publication of the Major Project and no more that five years, after which the data will be destroyed.

A copy of the final report will be available online from Royal Roads University and through UMI/Proquest and the Theses Canada portal. It will be publicly accessible and access and distribution will be unrestricted.

You are not compelled to participate in this research project. If you do choose to participate, you are free to withdraw at any time without prejudice. Similarly, if you choose not to participate in this research project, this information will also be maintained in confidence.

Thank you for your consideration. Please respond to this email if you will participate in my research project.

Yours truly,

Nancy Eidsvik,

APPENDIX G: Questions for Focus Group #1

1. What do you like best about Rotary and the Rotary Club of Prince Rupert?

   If you could change one thing about Rotary or the Rotary Club of Prince Rupert, what would that be?

2. Can you provide examples of how the Rotary Club can best expand its volunteer services to the community? (Expand need not mean more.) Why do you believe these examples are beneficial to the community?

   How will these examples be beneficial to the Club and members?

3. How can the Club improve the current method of selecting recipients for funding or service?

   How can the public be made aware of these funding opportunities?

4. How can members' involvement with the Club functions and activities be improved?

5. What is your perception of the satisfaction by the community of the services by the Rotary Club?

   What suggestions would you have to improve public knowledge of the Rotary Club?

6. Do you believe the needs of the members (the reason he or she joined Rotary) are being met? If so how; and if not, why?

APPENDIX H: Letter of Invitation to a World Cafe

Date: xxxxx, xx, 2007

Dear Members of the Rotary Club of Prince Rupert

I would like to invite you to be part of a research project that I am conducting. This project is part of the requirement for a Master's Degree in Leadership, at Royal Roads University. My name is Nancy Eidsvik and my credentials with Royal Roads University can be established by calling Dr. Gerry Nixon, Acting Director, School of Leadership Studies, at xx xxx xxxx or emailing xxxxxx@xxxxx.xx

The objective of my research project is to obtain your input as to how your view the volunteer services provided to the community by the Rotary Club of Prince Rupert and what you can suggest to best expand these services. The sponsoring organization for this project is the Rotary Club of Prince Rupert. In addition to submitting my final report to Royal Roads University in partial fulfillment for a Master's Degree in Leadership, I will also be sharing my research findings with the Rotary Club of Prince Rupert. The information (data) will be used for my Major Project Thesis.

My research project will consist of a World Café and is expected to last approximately one (1.0) hour during the regular Thursday Rotary meeting. The foreseen questions will refer to the volunteer services provided to the community by the Rotary Club of Prince Rupert and what you can suggest to best expand these services.

As members of the Rotary Club of Prince Rupert, I am seeking your input as it is your club and it is your input that is important to my research. I will be providing you the proposed questions at the World Cafe meeting as I wish to encourage spontaneous input.

Information will be recorded by the assigned groups and where appropriate summarized, in anonymous format, in the body of the final report. At no time will any specific comments be attributed to any individual unless your specific agreement has been obtained beforehand. All documentation will be kept strictly confidential.

A copy of the final report will be published. A copy will be housed at Royal Roads University, available online through UMI/Proquest and the Theses Canada portal and will be publicly accessible. Access and distribution will be unrestricted.

Please feel free to contact me at any time should you have additional questions regarding the project and its outcomes. If it is your preference, I will provide the contents of the notes regarding the focus group discussions and will be available to discuss and of the questions you may have regarding this meeting and/or its contents.

I do not perceive any conflict of interest as it is you the members who will be proving the input in written for at the World Café.

You are not compelled to participate in this research project. If you do choose to participate, you are free to withdraw at any time without prejudice. Similarly, if you choose not to participate in this research project, this information will also be maintained in confidence.

If you would like to participate in my research project, please contact me:
Name: Nancy Eidsvik
Email: xxxxx@xxxxx.xxx
Telephone: (xxx) xxx xxxx

Sincerely,

Nancy Eidsvik

APPENDIX I: World Café Agenda

Welcome to the Rotary Club's World Café

Agenda:

12:15 Call meeting to order

12:30 Discussions

12:40 Change tables

12:50 Change tables

1:00 Report to the group

1:15 End of World Café

APPENDIX J: World Café Questions

1. What do you like best about Rotary and the Rotary Club of Prince Rupert?

    If you could change one thing about Rotary or the Rotary Club of Prince Rupert, what would that be?

2. Can you provide examples of how the Rotary Club can best expand its volunteer services to the community? (Expand need not mean more.)

    Why do you believe these examples are beneficial to the community?

    How will these examples be beneficial to the club and members?

3. How can the Club improve the current method of selecting recipients for funding or service?

    How can the public be made aware of these funding opportunities?

4. How can members' involvement with the Club functions and activities be improved?

5. What is your perception of the satisfaction by the community of the services by the Rotary Club?

   What suggestions would you have to improve public knowledge of the Rotary Club?

6. Do you believe the needs of the members (the reason he or she joined Rotary) are being met? If so how; and if not, why?

APPENDIX K: Invitations to One-on-One Interviews

October 15, 2007

Members of the City Council
City of Prince Rupert

Dear Councillor

I would like to invite you to participate in my research project that I am conducting. This project is part of the requirement for a Master of Arts degree in Leadership and Training, at Royal Roads University. My credentials with Royal Roads University can be established by calling Dr. Gerry Nixon, Acting Director, School of Leadership Studies, at xxx xxx xxxx or emailing xxxx@xxxxxxx.xx

My interest in this research project is the result of my years with the Rotary Club of Prince Rupert. I have served as a director for four years and then as Secretary for almost five years. I became President and served from 2004 to 2005, served as past President, and then served as Treasurer from 2006 to 2007.

The objective of my research project is to obtain your input as to how you view the volunteer services provided to the community by the Rotary Club of Prince Rupert and what you can suggest to best expand these services. The sponsoring organization for this project is the Rotary Club of Prince Rupert. In addition to submitting my final report to Royal Roads University in partial fulfillment for a Master of Arts degree in Leadership and Training. I will also be sharing my research findings with the Rotary Club of Prince Rupert. The information (data) will be used for my Major Project Thesis.

My research project will consist of an Interview and is expected to last approximately one half (1/2) hour. The foreseen questions will refer to the volunteer services provided to the community by the Rotary Club of Prince Rupert and what you can suggest to best expand these services.

As members of the City Council of Prince Rupert, I am seeking your input at any time that is mutually convenient between the dates of October 22 and November 16, 2007. I will **not** be providing the questions in advance as I wish to encourage spontaneous input.

Information will be recorded by handwritten notes and, where appropriate summarized, in anonymous format, in the body of the final report. I can discuss the contents of my notes after the interview or I can provide you with a copy of the notes within a few days. At no time will any specific comments be attributed to any individual unless your specific agreement has been obtained beforehand. All documentation will be kept strictly confidential.

A copy of the final report will be available online from Royal Roads University, and through UMI/Proquest and the Theses Canada portal. It will be publicly accessible and access and distribution will be unrestricted.

Please feel free to contact me at any time should you have additional questions regarding the project and its outcomes. If it is your preference, I will provide the contents of the notes regarding the interview and I will be available to discuss any of the questions you may have regarding this meeting and/or its contents.

You are not compelled to participate in this research project. If you do choose to participate, you are free to withdraw at any time without prejudice. Similarly, if you choose not to participate in this research project, this information will also be maintained in confidence.

If you would like to participate in my research project, please contact me:

Name: Nancy Eidsvik

Email: xxxx@xxxxxxx.xx

Telephone: (xxx) xxx xxxx

Sincerely,

Nancy Eidsvik

APPENDIX L: One-on-One Interview Questions

Proposed questions to ask the City Council Members and selected administrative staff:

1. What do you perceive as the value Rotary brings to the community? Do you have any sense of the satisfaction by the Community?

2. What would you like to see Rotary do for the community?

3. How can Rotary's volunteer services assist the City of Prince Rupert?

4. Please suggest any other activities that could expand Rotary's volunteer services to the community.

5. Can you suggest how the Rotary Club can improve the current method of selecting recipients for funding or service? If so, what would your suggestions be?

APPENDIX M: Questions for Focus Group #2

1. How should the two Rotary Clubs work together—what should the process be?

2. What projects, events, or services should the two Rotary Clubs partner?

3. How do you think the Rotary Club of Prince Rupert can best expand its volunteer services to the community?

APPENDIX N: Letter of Invitation to Participate in the Survey

Nancy Eidsvik,

xxx xxx xxx

xxxx xxxxx xx xxx xxx

November 17, 2007

Name of Organization or individual

Dear

I would like to invite your organization to be part of a research project that I am conducting. This project is part of the requirement for my Master of Arts degree in Leadership and Training, at Royal Roads University. My credentials with Royal Roads University can be established by calling Dr. Gerry Nixon, Acting Director, School of Leadership Studies, at xxx xxx xxxx or emailing xxxxxxxx@xxxx.xx.

My interest in this research project is the result of my years with the Rotary Club of Prince Rupert. I have served as a director for four years and then as Secretary for almost five years. I became President and served from 2004 to 2005, served as past President, and then served as Treasurer from 2006 to 2007.

The objective of my research project is to obtain your input as to how you view the volunteer services provided to the community by the Rotary Club of Prince Rupert and what you can suggest to best expand these services. The sponsoring organization for this project is the Rotary Club of Prince Rupert. In addition I will be submitting my final report to Royal Roads University in partial fulfillment for a Master of Arts degree in Leadership and Training. I will also be sharing my research findings with the Rotary Club of Prince Rupert. The information (data) will be used for my Major Project Thesis.

My research project will consist of a survey is expected to take you not more that one half (1/2) hour. The foreseen questions will refer to the volunteer services provided to the community by the Rotary Club of Prince Rupert and what you can suggest to best expand these services.

As you are an active community organization in Prince Rupert, it is important that I obtain input from those outside of the Rotary Club of Prince Rupert as to how the Rotary Club is perceived in the community.

The information from the survey will be appropriately summarized, in anonymous format, in the body of the final report. At no time will any specific comments be attributed to any individual unless your specific agreement has been obtained beforehand. All documentation will be kept strictly confidential.

A copy of the final report will be available online from Royal Roads University and through UMI/Proquest and the Theses Canada portal. It will be publicly accessible and access and distribution will be unrestricted.

Please feel free to contact me at any time should you have additional questions regarding the project and its outcomes.

You are not compelled to participate in this research project. If you do choose to participate, you are free to withdraw at any time without prejudice. Similarly, if you choose not to participate in this research project, this information will also be maintained in confidence.

If you would like to participate in my research project, please contact me:

Name: Nancy Eidsvik xxxx@xxxx.xxx

Phone: (xxx)xxx xxxx

Sincerely,

Nancy Eidsvik

APPENDIX O: Letter of Acknowledgement to Participate in the Survey and Questions

November 20, 2007

Dear:

Thank you for agreeing to participate as the representative of your organization in my research project that I am conducting.

A copy of the final report will be available online from royal Roads University, and through UMI Proquest and the Theses Canada portal. It will be publicly accessible and access and distribution will be unrestricted.

You are not compelled to participate in this research project. If you do choose to participate, you are free to withdraw at any time without prejudice. Similarly, if you choose not to participate in this research project, this information will also be maintained in confidence. Approximately twenty organizations within Prince Rupert have been invited to participate and all those who accept will be sent the survey questions by their choice of email or mail.

The completion and return or submission of this survey gives me the permission I require to use the information to prepare my research project, "How can the Rotary Club of Prince Rupert best expand its volunteer services to the community?" The sponsoring organization is the Rotary Club of Prince Rupert. At no time will any specific comments be attributed to any individual. Anonymous quotations may be used in the final report in addition to the summarized information. All documentation will be kept strictly confidential and will be destroyed to ensure confidentially.

You may place your comments directly on this survey and email it back to me to ensure it will be kept confidential upon receipt. I would appreciate the return before November 15, 2007.

Name: Nancy Eidsvik

Email: neidsvik@community.royalroads.ca

Telephone: (xxx)xxx xxxx

Thank you very much,

Nancy Eidsvik

Survey Questions for Community Service Provider Organizations.

Wherever possible, please respond from the perspective of your organization

1. Are you aware of what Rotary does for the community and its goals?
   If so, what do you believe that Rotary does?

2. What would you like to see Rotary do for the community?

3. How can Rotary be of service to you?

4. Can you suggest how the Rotary Club should select the recipients for funding or service? If so, what would your suggestions be?

5. Please suggest any other activities that could expand Rotary's volunteer services to the community.
6. What is your opinion of the community's satisfaction of the community services offered by the Rotary Club?

7. Have you been involved with Rotary in the past? If so, what was your experience?

8. What interests you about volunteer service, and what reasons do you have to become involved?

9. Any other comments you wish to make.